"Reading Megan's debut book feels a lot like the time I first met her in person. My heart sings, 'My friend! I've found her!' and my body relaxes in the relief that I can be myself around her. She has a long history with the Lord, which serves only to benefit us—her readers, her friends. Megan's faith is pure and beautiful and bold and honest. She is not just a ray of light or a breath of fresh air—she is the whole sunrise and the ocean breeze that wakes us up—bringing us hope and fresh space to move into and occupy. She calls us out of the pits we've fallen into (willingly or not) and she does so with the joy and humor of the Lord. Seriously, she is so funny.

I am married with young kids, so I don't 'belong' to the unmarried audience to whom Megan gives voice—but that's the beauty of her testimony—Megan's sharing of faith and Biblical truth transcends the categories of belonging our culture is so obsessed with putting everyone into. She gives us all the gift of the simple gospel—freeing us from the confines and false security of titles and allowing us to walk in the joy and adventure of who God created us to be—exactly where we're at in life."

—**Kate Kiesel,** *I Would Live for You,* Punchline Publishing

"How does a single woman thrive in the marriage culture of today's church? Megan E. Faulkner answers that question with authenticity as she shares her journey of using God's truth to replace the lie that she's 'not enough.' She's practical, funny, honest, and upbeat, and she gives a great checklist at the end of each chapter on how to flourish as a single woman of God in a married world. Her easy-to-read, welcoming style will inform, encourage, and challenge all women, single or married."

—**Warren Bird,** Author/Coauthor of 34 books including
Hero Maker, Zondervan, and Michelle Zwicker Bird,
Leader for 30 years of women's Bible studies and discipleship

"Megan Faulkner didn't want to write this book. But God . . . She had been in the pit. But God . . . She was deconstructing what she thought she didn't have. But God . . . She was living in what-was-supposed-to-be for too long. But God . . . Megan is telling her own story with such honesty, vulnerability and authenticity and a huge healthy dose of humor. All the while allowing us, the readers, to realize we have our own stories to tell, stories that can be filled with purpose because God is present."

—**Maggie Robbins,** Co-author with Duffy Robbins of
Enjoy the Silence, Zondervan, and Certified Spiritual Director

"Have you ever felt incomplete just as you are? Then this book is for you. Megan beautifully invites readers to grapple with the deep questions of our God-given purpose in a world that constantly throws comparison, hopelessness, and fear at us. She invites us to step into the freedom bought through the precious blood of Jesus Christ in a way that will make you laugh and cry. This book will change you for the better."

—**Jenna Shotmeyer,** Author *Are You Drowning? Overcoming in the Midst of Trauma and Loss*

"In an engaging, meaningful and creative manner, this book offers incredible encouragement to single women of all ages. Megan's personal stories and gems from the Bible show how to transform pitfalls into purpose, revealing secrets to living the best life regardless of expectations or relational status."

—**Pastor Raphael and Aly Giglio,** *Soul or the Spirit: Knowing the Difference Can Change Your Life*

HAPPILY
EVER
After All

On-Purpose Living in a Fairytale World

MEGAN E. FAULKNER

Print ISBN: 979-8-9868023-6-7
Digital ISBN: 979-8-9868023-7-4
LCCN: LCCN: 2023903809

Cover and Interior Design by Nelly Murariu at PixBeeDesigns.com
Manuscript Edits by Ariel Curry Editorial and Market Refined Media, LLC
Author headshot by Raymond Morton Photography

Printed in the United States of America
First Edition: May 2023

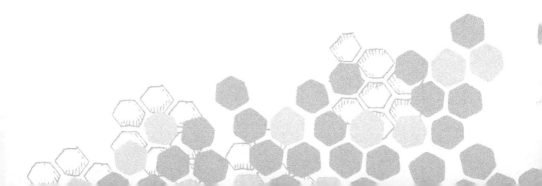

To my Mom and Dad, who believe in my dreams more than I do.
Some things are wildly unrelenting, and
your love is at the top of that list. I love you!

To Hailey, Evelyn, Nicholas, and their parents,
While Author is a title I've dreamt of forever,
Sister and Aunt will always beat it.
You are my favorite people. I love you!

To every girl who has cried on her bathroom floor,
I know that ache.
This is for you.

Contents

INTRODUCTION

Love and Other Stories

I did not want to write this book. How's that for an opener? In fact, I had an entirely different story line in my head, an outline written out, and a lot of the book that I did want to write already accomplished. Even in this, I'm not getting my way. (Have you ever felt that way in your life? Maybe that's why you're reading this right now.) I'm just simply not getting my way. If I were a toddler, I would be throwing a temper tantrum in the middle of the grocery aisle; but my toddler days are long gone and I don't currently have one of those either—a toddler, that is. So here I am: thirty-something, unmarried, and no toddler. What good am I to the world? Are you in the same boat? Have you ever thought—*what good am I to the world*? That's why we're all here: to figure it out together. I'm glad you're here.

Here's what I want to tell you most before anything else: being unmarried is not an affliction. (Just so we're all on the same page.) No one needs to feel sorry for the unmarried women—we're fine. We're not dying; we're living, or well, we're trying to—if people would let us. *Yikes, right?* Well, just hear me out. The unending questions and comments from married people in Christian culture such as *"Don't you want to be married already?" "Why aren't you married yet?"* and *"The clock is ticking*!" echo in the walls of our heads for days after they're said to us.

The truth is that there is a purpose in everything and that's what we're here to discover. What is the purpose in each of these situations we find ourselves in as unmarried women in Christian culture?

Rachel and Ross. Jay Z and Beyonce. Steph and Alicia Curry. John Legend and Chrissy Teigen. Viola Davis and Julius Tennon. Noah and Allie. Corey and Topanga. Phil and Claire. Blake Lively and Ryan Reynolds. All stories of love and marriage, and sometimes babies. People whose stories our society has collectively grown to love, follow, and adore. Christians have our own versions of these stories: Isaac and Rebecca, Jacob and Rachel, Ruth and Boaz, your pastor and their spouse, and many other famous Christian couples we follow starry-eyed, thinking that's *exactly* how it's supposed to happen. Some of us dream, hope, and pray for a similarly great story one day.

But for many of us, it doesn't happen. Life doesn't look how we thought it should look, and our stories are drastically different from the ones we read about in fairytales. We begin comparing our lives to our friends' lives and wonder what is wrong with us. Everyone is getting married and having babies while we're still in the same place we've been for an exceptionally long time, or so it seems. Their highlight reels begin to take center stage in our minds while we muck through the reality of our behind-the-scenes. We get trapped in making comparisons, and the self-judgment feels like a never-ending roller coaster. We get stuck in the vicious cycle of thinking about what they have and what we don't. Our stories are ever evolving, but we're not certain they're evolving the way we want them to. We compare the purpose of our lives and feel behind, lost, hopeless, and maybe even stuck.

The comparison trap is one of the greatest traps of all time. Comparing our lives to the lives of others often robs us of our joy, disillusions us with the reality of disappointed expectations, makes us feel unsatisfied with our current place in life, and communicates lies to our hearts that can take root and leave us tangled. The comparison trap is just that: a trap. A trap is *a trick by which someone is misled into acting contrary to their interests or intentions,* or *an unpleasant situation from which it is hard to escape.* Comparison traps us into thinking we've done something wrong, or, worse yet, *we* are wrong. The lies that comparison communicates are the opposite of the things God wants for us, especially when it comes to our life's purpose. Another way we can think of comparison is as a pitfall. It's something that catches us, buries us, and is difficult to escape from without some hard work.

Freedom is on the other side of the pitfall of comparison. While comparison lies say things like, "You're not where you're supposed to be," God combats those lies with sentiments like, "I have every one of your steps numbered and I am with you always." I know so many of us struggle with believing the lies that come from the mouth of the comparison trap. It's a dangerous place to try to receive our information and validation. The mouth of God is the only place to receive our true identity. God says that we are loved, chosen, accepted, wanted by Him, redeemed, and created for a purpose.

God's Word, the Bible, is filled with stories of women and men whose lives each looked drastically different from others'. No two stories are the same, yet we continue to draw our own parallels to the lives of our friends and neighbors in this modern day. As Christians, we are called to live in freedom and to do so abundantly. Abundant free living doesn't look like comparing ourselves to our friends, and it certainly doesn't only exist within the construct of marriage. Abundant and free living looks like being surrendered to Jesus, the Savior of the world, and seeking the will of God regularly. A life of abundance and a life of freedom doesn't come from reaching the world's social goals of marriage and children; it comes from living a beautiful life surrendered to a God who loves us, cares for us, and has better plans for our lives than we could ever make up for ourselves. It seems to be that everybody thinks unmarried Christian women are incomplete, but that's not true—we are fully complete because of Jesus, wholly alive, and purposed for greatness.

Living a great story does not only look like a husband, two kids, a white picket fence, and a dog. It doesn't look like being a billionaire or even a millionaire. Living a great story doesn't look like the perfect car, the perfect haircut (*did I go a little too far?*), or the perfect job. What does it look like to you? I think it looks like training for the most epic race of your life with skinned up knees, bruises, scars, and bright-eyed smiles. It smells like summer rain, spring flowers, winter fires, and fall hayrides. It feels like sand under your feet, freshly cut grass, and holding the hand of someone you adore. It tastes like cold ice cream on a hot summer day, like hot coffee on the coldest morning, and like the best pizza on this side of the Mississippi. It sounds like the good kind of laughter—you know the one I'm talking about, the one from your belly. It sounds like silence to the ones who like the quiet and noise to the ones who don't. It looks big and bright and bold and beautiful, and it's reflective of calling and persistence and kindness and goodness. It feels holy, and faithful, and slow, and right. Living a great story looks like whatever each of our individual stories are—not just a cookie cutter calling. My story is not yours, and your story is not mine—and isn't that what's so beautifully wild about it all? We're not the same. We're not called to sameness—and that's why this book exists. I had this ache of shame because I was not the same. The shame lied to me, it held me back, and it didn't let me *live*.

Simply put, a great story is one filled with purpose. And friend, purpose is something you do have. We'll continue to talk about purpose in each chapter, and hopefully we'll be encouraged along the way that our stories are *good*—regardless of our marital status.

This Book is for You

If you're unmarried and reading this book: Welcome, friend! I'm glad you're here. This is for you. No, really, it's *for* you. I want you to feel the freedom to say things that maybe no one has said before, or that maybe no one has given you the freedom to express prior to this message. In this book, friend, I pray you find that freedom. I pray these pages sink into your bones; your heart swells in size; and you feel seen, known, loved, and heard. You matter to the world. You have a purpose here, and I'm glad we're here together.

I'm not sure what lies you've heard or are believing, or what words said by others have etched their way into the walls of your heart, but the prayer for this book is that you will find hope and purpose here. Your marital status, dating status, or any other status for that matter, have very little—or absolutely nothing—to do with your purpose. You don't have more or less purpose because of your marital status; you have purpose today simply because there is breath in your lungs and your heart is still beating.

Looking Ahead

Each chapter ahead is written as a letter to you to help you navigate your purpose in that specific facet of life. You'll read stories, gain some wisdom, and hopefully feel seen, known, and heard! We'll talk about a pitfall in the respective situation and then move towards climbing out of that thinking and shifting our perspective to purpose. Then—something fun!

My friend Kelly and I love lists. She's one of the only other people in the entire universe whose lists I know rival mine. We especially love a checklist. We started running together and each time we run, we give ourselves a checkmark. We eventually decided we also needed prizes; now things that bring us joy come into play after we gain so many checkmarks on our lists. If our goal is to *thrive,* not just survive, in this culture where we live, we're going to need to check some things off our list. We cannot sit still and expect change. We must take action and move forward; and sometimes, making lists can help! At the end of each chapter, you'll find a checklist. Use the checklist to your advantage. I've tried to make them practical for you, but also fun. I'm not doing much without fun.

While the journey through these pages might bring up some uncomfortable feelings and initiate some difficult conversations, we're going to have fun together in the in-between. Maybe you'll cry, but maybe you'll also laugh. Most of all, I hope you'll feel free. Check it off, sister! (Kelly recommends prizes!)

Here are all the letters to all the unmarried women in all the situations where you find yourself: may they reach you, meet you, and fill you with hope. It is time for us to live abundantly and to live free. It is time for the chains of comparison to fall to the wayside and the pitfalls to become purposeful so we can live out our callings free of the shame that comparison brings. It's time for women to be valued socially and in the Church regardless of our marital status or ability to reproduce. It's time to live in expectation of *what* is next, not *who* is next. It's time, because who says a happily ever after that includes a spouse is the goal, after all?

CHAPTER 1

Stuck in the Pit

PITFALL THINKING
If I'm in the pit now, I'll always be
in the pit. This is just my life.

PURPOSE THINKING
I can make progress toward living
an abundant, purposeful life.

Sweet friend,

Have you ever heard of the Greatest Commandment? If you haven't, it reads something like this:

> "Hearing that Jesus had silenced the Sadducees, the Pharisees got together. One of them, an expert in the law, tested him with this question: 'Teacher, which is the greatest commandment in the Law?' Jesus replied: 'Love the Lord your God with all your **heart** and with all your **soul** and with all your **mind.**'[c] This is the first and greatest commandment. And the second is like it: 'Love your neighbor as yourself.'[d] All the Law and the Prophets hang on these two commandments." Matthew 22:34-40 NIV

I want to tell you why this commandment is so important to our lives in this season. But first, a story:

It was the hottest day to date in July and I was carefully picking up tiny shards of broken glass. A vase had fallen from a corner cabinet and shattered, sending glass to every inch of my sink and the surrounding countertops. The house was quiet except for me, joyfully laughing, picking up each tiny piece. It doesn't seem like a scenario in which to laugh unless you're me; this is how I knew I was healed and free, finally living my purpose.

If this same scenario had played out just two years prior, I would have left the glass there and not used my sink for the foreseeable future. I would have pretended like it was going to magically clean itself up and ignored it entirely. That flawed thinking had become my battle cry: *This isn't happening, this can't be happening. This is just my life. I will be in this pit forever!* I had been through some seasons that felt like torture, and therefore, I began to suppress, isolate, ignore, and surrender to a life of depression. I was stuck.

Maybe you've felt stuck in that pitfall before, or maybe you're stuck now, and your sink is full of tiny shards of glass waiting to be cleaned up. Have you had a hard time making a decision? Can't decide where to go next on a project or a dream? Have you given up on something you know was for you, or at least, you thought was for you? Is your life mundane, systematic, and repetitive? Does your mind dictate your next move, not allowing the heart any input? Are you stuck in a career, stuck in a mindset, stuck in a pattern of thinking that isn't free, stuck in a cycle of toxicity, stuck in your own way? Friend, this is a problem, but we can climb out together. Let's keep going.

STUCK; 1. adjective; *caught or fixed* as in "stuck in the mud."
2. adjective; *baffled*

"This problem has me completely stuck." *Stuck describes something that's frozen or fixed in one place and can't be moved. If your foot gets stuck in the mud, it means you can't get your foot out of its messy trap. The lid of a jar can be stuck, and your car can get stuck in traffic; either way, the thing that's stuck isn't going anywhere. You can also use stuck when you can't figure out what to do: you can be stuck on an especially hard math problem or feel stuck in a complicated relationship.*

Stuck. Dwelling somewhere we shouldn't. Past tense. No movement. Unable to proceed. Fixed in place.

We are not meant to live stuck in the pit. We are created to live free.

When we surrender to God's ultimate design for each of our lives, freedom becomes the supreme battle cry. When we can shift one foot out of the cement holding us in place and toward movement, *stuck* doesn't get the majority of the say. If we can seek healing, reframe our thinking, and remember our dreams, being stuck becomes a thing of the past and progress towards purpose becomes our medal.

Your stuck might not seem important to move out of quickly; but maybe you're stuck on your next move. Maybe you love your career but want to make progress towards excellence. Maybe you're stuck in a relational decision and need to work it through, or you're stuck in an unhealthy family or work system that you want to help guide toward movement. I think if we're not careful, we can all be stuck in, or on, something. My stuck was not a stuck I ever imagined or asked for, knew how to deal with, or understood.

I was fixed, alright—perhaps even fixated. Why could I not accomplish this goal of marriage that was set before me by, well, just about everyone in my world? Why did I feel less-than because others' expectations of my life were not being met? Or was it that my expectations for my own life were also not being met? Why was everyone so obsessed with finding someone to share their life with and not just building a life they were proud of? Or was I also obsessed with it? When we're in this situation, our lives can become constant discussions and suggestions around the next right suitor, and the *"what happened"* discussions fill the airwaves after dates or even a match on a dating app! It's no wonder we feel left behind if we're not accomplishing these goals. We're not the only ones obsessed with the goal of relationship—everyone around us seemingly is, too!

I was stuck alone, everywhere, and the pain of that loneliness forced me to face some really hard questions.

Who told you everyone gets married?

Why is that the goal in life?

Who decided that the married way is the only way to live a fulfilled life?

It was a painful reckoning, and one that still requires revisiting sometimes—reminding myself and encouraging others through.

Back to the Vase

Why was it a situation in which to laugh? Because *pitfall thinking Megan* would have left the shattered glass right there, not dealing with one more thing that wasn't going my way. But I laughed, and I noticed the laugh. Why? Because *purpose-thinking Megan* had finally arrived on the scene. I was healed from being stuck in the pit, and I knew it based on my willing-to-clean-up-the-vase-right-away actions.

Late 2020, three months after laughing over the shattered vase, I woke up on an early fall Saturday morning to an incredible view. My two best friends and I spent a Friday night in the Pocono Mountains in Pennsylvania catching our collective breath. We branded it as "Megan's Birthday Party," which was celebrated with all my favorite things. But we all like the same stuff anyway, so it worked out for everyone, I think!

We spent time laughing; sharing stories; reliving college days, high school days, and even childhood days; eating too much charcuterie; and sitting in the hot tub splashing around like we were twelve. It was soul-nourishing.

I drove home Saturday afternoon, the first day of my new year of life, full of happiness and also lots of cheese. (They're the same thing, no?)

I do not know a lot, but this is what I do know: not one soul in the world thought these years would go how they're going. Who imagined a global pandemic, political chaos, overwhelmingly tense feelings everywhere you go, immense racial inequality in America coming to the surface needing to be confronted, and a toilet paper shortage? And for me—and maybe you, too—I navigated it mostly alone. I didn't process these years in the quiet of the night with anyone as we waited to fall asleep. I just had my own thoughts—and maybe a few texts. I never imagined it would be this way.

I drove along the highway home—reliving the past year of my life, celebrating the victories, and sobbing at the sadness. That's right, I cry hard and drive carefully. *See me for multitasking tips and tricks!* I experienced incredible pain that year, but I also experienced the freedom that comes with healing. The drive home allowed me to think through the processes that made me into who I was that very day, celebrate doing the hard work of seeking vision, creating a close and prayerful circle of confidants, and making decisions that simultaneously broke my heart and set me free. My heart was breaking for the life I thought I was going to have, yet didn't, and that brokenness also set me free into the life and purpose I could now pursue.

This is what I know: I am okay. This was the conclusion of my drive home from the mountains. While this might not sound like a big deal to you, I had lived the previous four years of my life thinking I may never be okay again. I had battled—and I mean, *battled*—some mean beasts; all while being entrusted with ministries, domestic and foreign; creating community; reframing my thinking about a life I thought I was going to have by now; and trying to just make it through the day. In seeking healing, I received it. I have never felt more happy, free, and confident in my life. I was healed and whole; my battle had been won.

I began to work hard. I begged, pleaded, prayed, journaled, and read. I saw the most incredible Christian therapist, had difficult conversations, sought forgiveness, forgave, and reconciled. I worked hard to eliminate ego, increased my time with God, rearranged my schedule, incorporated a true Sabbath and protected it. I set boundaries and kept them and started telling the whole truth. The journey to this healing started when my pastor/boss walked into my office one day eighteen months prior and said, "I don't know how to ask you this, but are you okay?" I sobbed. "No," I replied. "But I don't know why." He sat and listened, prayed for me, and said, "However I can support you, just tell me." Those became the eight most important words after "Do you want to know Jesus?" of my whole life.

Most of my adulthood has felt like big dreams realized and big dreams s h a t t e r e d, sometimes all at once. I have experienced incredibly high highs and some of the lowest of lows of my life, but I am okay. Why? Because even when I didn't deserve it, Jesus showed up for me. He arrived in the form of friends and neighbors, bright sunny days and blue skies, time alone with Him, and fresh pages of a journal. We are quick to run to the things we think will make us feel better: money, relationships, notoriety, social media likes, power, food—the list could go on. But God . . . nothing can heal the things that are meant for only Him to heal. He brought me right out of the pit and into a purposeful life with Him. Just as in Psalm 40:2, David writes: *"He lifted me out of the slimy pit, out of the mud and mire; he set my feet on a rock and gave me a firm place to stand."*

He is waiting for us to seek His will, His desires, and His plans for our lives. Often while we're busy crying in the corner, wondering why things aren't going well, we realize we hadn't invited Him into them in the first place.

Back to the greatest commandment—this, my sweet friend, is our whole life's purpose. The purpose of life is not to be married; the purpose of life is to love the Lord our God with all of our heart, soul, mind, and strength, and to love our neighbor as we love ourselves. When we are stuck, it is seemingly impossible to accomplish this. Being married is not the end-all and be-all of life; obedience is. Jesus came for us so we could have life and have it abundantly. Staying stuck does not produce abundance. Furthermore, when we're stuck, it's almost impossible to love our neighbors well because we don't necessarily love ourselves well. We try to love ourselves well, but we end up loving ourselves with our broken heart, and a wounded soul, and a tormented mindmind—and then we love our neighbors through that lens. If we're not healed and whole and loving ourselves well, it is incredibly hard to live out our purpose in its fullness and love our neighbors well, too. So, if we can seek healing for our stuck-ness, if we're looking to get out from the traps and pitfalls, if we can live in a place with the Lord where we are engaging in abundant love with our hearts and souls and mind, we can love our neighbors better, because we love ourselves as He loves us.

I've spent most of my adult life living in resentment and feeling left. Maybe you've felt the same way? My friends were marrying the people of their dreams, creating the cutest families ever known to earth, and purchasing white picket fences (quite literally!). I grew up thinking that's what I always wanted for two reasons: that's what I was told I wanted and that's what I did want! I still want to be married and have my own family—truly, it is the only thing I feel like I don't have in life—but now I will only pursue that path if it's the obedient and right thing to do. I am so done fighting God on this. It's exhausting. He always wins, and I always cry. I've spent the last four years deconstructing what I thought I didn't have and realizing what I do.

Through the wise counsel of my team at work, the epic questions from an amazing Christian therapist, and the constant support of my family and best friends, I've been able to realize that I've hit some home runs in life while I thought I was just sitting on the bench! What freedom is in that realization. I haven't been benched at all; I've been batting and swinging and hitting and running and accomplishing things for the Team that I wouldn't have been able to otherwise. In regaining perspective, I was able to surrender, to rid myself of resentments and to see the joy once again in this epic journey.

I'm wondering if you're in need of the encouragement of surrender today. Are you holding onto things that weren't meant for you? Are you clinging to a life that isn't yet, instead of surrendering to a life of what could be? Are you operating on your own timeline or the timeline the world puts on you? I lived in what was supposed-to-be for so long I missed out on what-is-now. I don't want you to miss out, too.

Author and podcaster Annie F. Downs once wrote in an Instagram caption: "In the musical *Les Mis[erables]*, Fantine sings a song that says, ' . . . now life has killed the dream I dreamed.' *(She had just been fired from her job at the factory and thrown onto the streets. Things were not going exactly according to her plan. She is thinking back to happier days and she's wondering how everything has gone wrong in her life.)* And in my story, that's been true a few times. (Yours too probably, right?) Big LIFE ones and 2020 ones and little daily ones. But when the song stops, our lives don't, and also? That song doesn't factor in God's kindness. Your life, your year, may not look the way you thought it would (mine either!) some dreams may have died, but some new dreams have grown . . . and there's SO MUCH FUN when you are given what you didn't know to dream up."

My encouragement for you today, friend, is to be open to the dreams God has for you—the ones you don't even know about: the married ones and the unmarried ones, the career ones and the personal ones, the social ones, and the emotional ones. I didn't think I would find my dreams again on these past few trips around the sun, but I did, and it's been better than I could have ever imagined. There is freedom in surrender, peace in absolute uncertainty, and calm in the chaos if we choose it.

I want to challenge you today to:

... see your dreams,

... find the peace amidst the storm,

... seek Jesus instead of whatever else you're looking to for satisfaction,

... ask for healing where you need to be healed,

... commit to a process of betterment if you're in the pit,

... and to choose to see, or actively look for, the joy in the journey.

He is here waiting for you. Will you submit to Him today? In this book? Through these letters? Will you let go of whatever is causing you angst and admit that His plans are best? Will you choose to surrender, to open your hand, and to reimagine what a life full of Him could look like? This reimagining brings us back to the purpose of our lives: loving Him and loving others. Let's turn the page and walk through this beautiful life together, thriving. Let's start at the very beginning. You can make progress toward living an abundant, stuck-free life.

I promise it's good.
It's not always pretty.
But it *is* always good.

Let's get started,
Megan

ESCAPING THE PIT CHECKLIST

◇ Decide to get out of the pit. (Picking this book up is a good start!)

◇ Call a trusted friend to tell them you're in the pit.

◇ Decide what ONE thing you will do this week to gain forward movement.

◇ Write out (or talk through, if you're braver than me!) a list of resentments you're holding onto.

◇ Take a walk and drink some water.

CHAPTER 2

Little Girls' Dreams

PITFALL THINKING

In order to live a fulfilled life,
I must get married.

PURPOSE THINKING

God has numbered my days
and my steps. His plans for me
are perfect plans.

Hey Dreamer,

Can I tell you how much Jesus loves you? Do you want to know what He thought about you as a little girl? Look at this:

> "Then people brought little children to Jesus for him to place his hands on them and pray for them. But the disciples rebuked them. Jesus said, 'Let the little children come to me, and do not hinder them, for the kingdom of heaven belongs to such as these.' When he had placed his hands on them, he went on from there." Matthew 19:13-14 NIV

He loves, cherishes, encourages, and supports kids. He's asking the rulers of the day to let the children come to him, to sit with him, and to talk with him. He then gives specific instructions about what they are to do next: don't stop them from doing so. The Kingdom belongs to them—to us! When we are little, he says the entire Kingdom belongs to us. Do you know how many dreams we could dream if we let ourselves go there?

Take yourself back to your childhood and try to remember what kinds of things you imagined. Did you play baseball in the backyard to a stadium full of fans? Did you own a pet shop? Were you the best hair stylist in the world, creating new looks for clients all the time? Did you play house with an imaginary spouse and purchase a white picket fence and a dog? Did you dream of a world where every kid ate ice cream only for lunch? A world full of oceans and everyone was a mermaid? My dreams? Oh, I was the White House Press Secretary. Yes, I was. I held press conferences, answered questions, and created all sorts of microphones for myself to be heard. Looking back now, it was telling. I also was the CEO of a business my cousins and I ran out of the first level of my grandparents' home. I had a desk in the hall, and my cousins worked very hard in the living room. I think we were bankers; our Mom-Mom, the Mid-Atlantic jargon for Grandmother, worked at a bank, so it was the world we thought we knew. Boy, did we get a lot accomplished on those days! Immediately following our staff meetings, we jumped in the pool and ran around for hours on our breaks. We played on the swing set, helped shuck the corn or snap the peas for dinner, and then we were back to being bankers and CEOs. We dreamed big. No one stopped us, and the stapler was our best friend. We pushed papers back and forth all day long and everyone approved everything! It was a dream.

Dreamer, what did you dream about? Did you know then that the entire Kingdom could be yours?

We are no more than three years old when people start asking us questions about our futures. No one asks *who* we want to be when we grow up; they ask *what* we want to be. Quickly associating worth with contribution in our young minds, we decide what we want to do. We become dreamers looking forward to a life of being a doctor, lawyer, teacher, veterinarian, artist, and oftentimes, a mom. We are given baby dolls as gifts from the time we are barely more than infants ourselves. Shortly after the baby doll toy comes into play, we experience sentences like "When you get married and have a baby . . ." or "When you grow up and become a mommy . . ." or "You're going to be such a good wife . . ." *We're five! How do you know that?!* We're really focused on our goldfish and hula hoop at the moment, and I'm not sure those skills are transferable to wifehood. We are created for nurturing, but nurturing doesn't only come in the form of motherhood. Enter the pitfall. What happens when the life we've dreamed of doesn't seem to be coming true in real life?

From what I remember, I had an amazing childhood. I ran outside and played and climbed trees. I had tea parties, created mud pie factories, and rode my bike. I played dress up, hairdresser, and house. Maybe you did, too. I was outside for hours on end and I painted my nails a differ-ent color every other day. I was on the swim team, softball team and volleyball team; acted in the school plays; and danced for a few years at the same dance school. My closet held frilly dresses, pink shirts, and cleats with dried mud on them. I had a thousand ponytail holders all over the house at any given moment, and a sweet right hook ready to clock one of my brothers, should the need arise. I loved being outside, and I loved shopping with my mom. I loved cooking and making up clubs during elementary school recess, trying to get as many people included before the whistle blew to line up and go inside. I enjoyed professional sports and Broadway, and I also enjoyed traveling and staying home watching movies.

But the rhetoric I heard that sunk deep into my mind and heart at a very young age—from people I love, respect, and admire to this day—was less about who I was going to become, and more about what I was going to do. No one asked if I wanted to grow up to be kind, patient, loving, faithful, a leader, discerning, and spirited—they asked who I wanted to marry and what my kid's names would be. Fast forward to being thirty-something and unmarried . . . What do you think that does to a dreamer's soul who was supposed to have the Kingdom at her fingertips? No matter how hard I've tried, I haven't been able to accomplish this one dream that I, *and others*, dreamed for me. What am I supposed to do now?

Maybe you had a similar experience, where caring, kind, loving adults focused more on your *what* than your *who*. Many people experience similar feelings today, both outside and inside the context of marriage. We feel as though our worth is lessened because we're not a certain thing or we've never achieved a certain thing. What a trap!

I recently interviewed my dad for my podcast, *Wife Me Up*. As an aside, *Wife Me Up* was born out of a joke that came from sharing good things I created on my Instagram stories. I posted charcuterie boards, dinners, breakfast boards, and the like and suggested that somebody somewhere "wife me up!" I just could not understand how someone who could make something this good was without a husband! The podcast became a movement to create things for others to enjoy. We share lots of stories of people living in abundance and power and doing exactly what they're called to do—regardless of their relationship status.

When asking Dad about his relationship with his grandchildren (to date, he has three), he told me that he's so careful about how he speaks to them because he doesn't want to limit them in any way. He doesn't ask about future occupations; he asks about ideas and dreams. My heart almost exploded out of my chest. This is what we need to hear.

When we're adults, our titles can't define us. Our roles as sisters, wives, mothers, employees, friends, neighbors, and aunts are all good, but they're just that: roles we play. Who we are is different from what we do.

Who are you? Are you kind, compassionate, trustworthy, and funny?

What do you do? Are you a teacher, doctor, business owner, or personal trainer?

Who we are influences what we do. But they're not the same thing. Let's change how we speak to Jesus's little children, and maybe even ourselves. We don't know what's hanging in the balance, we don't know what impact we may be having on those children's future lives and dreams simply by how we speak to them. God still wants good things for us today because we belong to Him. We are His children, who He has dreams for, as well! I don't ever want to speak for God and be wrong, but in my own searching and wandering, I believe God is more concerned with who we are than what we do. I think He cares about the state of our heart, how we relate to Him, how we treat ourselves, and how we treat each other, more than what our occupation is or where we work.

This is why I think women, regardless of marital status, can be strong and vulnerable, confident and timid, have a servant heart, and tell someone "no" should the need arise. There's beauty in the middle ground of being and doing, and there are plenty more dreams in the Kingdom. When we hyper focus on the what, instead of the who, that's often where our dreams shatter and we are left in the pit.

When you think about your childhood, what conversations do you remember having? I recently surveyed a diverse group of unmarried women with this question. Interestingly, most of their answers were similar. Over 80% of the women surveyed noted their remembered childhood conversations centered around future occupation and marriage. Sentences like, "When you get married . . . " were noted being used often, and questions from caring adults such as, "What do you want to be when you grow up?" filled the conversation market. Specifically, the surveyed women noted their search for their own Prince Charming began at a young age. What happens next is unintentional, but incredibly painful for the inner child who later is unmarried by the time culture says she should be married. These questions and conversations we have with children often create an unfulfilled desire for people who are unmarried by the time society says they should be married. But what if it didn't have to be that way? What if our conversations with children were laced with potential and goodness, with kindness and betterment for the world? Sure, we should have healthy relational conversations with our children—but when we make the *what* the focus instead of the *who*, we are unintentionally perpetuating a cycle of shame.

Maybe you've felt similarly? Maybe you feel similarly right now and that's why you're reading this book. Dreamer, let's keep dreaming. Are we measuring ourselves against these initial questions of *who* God has called us to be, or are we measuring ourselves against who other people are?

What dreams do you have today? Let's get moving on them! We don't need to waste any time waiting. Who are you ready to be? Go be her. Do you dream of a life filled with kind words, beautiful thoughts, and the kind of hospitality that beckons people to be themselves around you? Do you dream about the future and the kind of person you will be when you're ninety-seven and sipping sweet tea in a rocking chair with your best friend? Who are your dreams calling you to be? Don't stop dreaming. Don't ever stop dreaming.

Because our marital status doesn't define us, I'm wondering if we can shift our pit perspective from the flawed thinking that living a married life is the only way to be who we are created to be into a purposeful perspective where living a life full of dreams for the kind of heart we want to have matters most. But first, let's root out the weeds. God has numbered your days and ordered your steps. His plans for you are perfect plans.

Keep dreaming,
Megan

LITTLE GIRLS' DREAMS CHECKLIST

◇ Write down your top five favorite attributes about yourself.

◇ Call a childhood friend or a family member and talk about your dreams as a little girl.

◇ Ask three trusted friends to describe your heart and mind in adjectives only.

◇ Write down one big dream you have for your life. Go nuts!

◇ Take a walk and drink some water.

CHAPTER 3

Shame

PITFALL THINKING

Because my life does not look how I thought it was going to look or how others thought it was *supposed* to look, something is wrong with me.

PURPOSE THINKING

I am carefully crafted in the image of God and have submitted my life to Jesus; therefore, I am enough.

Hey Free Bird,

Relax your jaw line, lower your shoulders, and take a deep breath. I know these conversations aren't exactly comfortable, but we have some good company in the Bible when it comes to having uncomfortable conversations! We don't know her name or age, but her conversation with Jesus is the longest recorded one-on-one chat in the Bible. This is a reason to give our friend from Samaria another look. It was the middle of the day, and Jesus, tired from traveling, carefully chose a place to stop and rest—Jacob's Well, which was right outside the town of Sychar—while he waited for his disciples to get food from town. Our Samaritan friend arrives on scene here with a jar, at the well, filling it with water. Jesus asks her a simple question: *"Will you give me a drink?"*

She responds, "Are you kidding me? You're a Jewish man and I'm a woman from Samaria! How can you even ask me such a question?" (John 4:7-9)

Representing the lowest of the low, the outcast of the outcasts, a female in society where women were disregarded and often demeaned, and from a culture that Jewish people historically wanted nothing to do with, she is bold enough to speak back to Jesus. That alone gives me enough curiosity to want to check her story out a little bit more.

Instead of insisting she pour him a drink, Jesus does something super weird for their day, and maybe even *today*! He offers her living water. What in the world is He talking about? She has no idea, but He certainly catches her attention. She is polite, but a little gutsy, and replies, "You have nothing to draw with and the well is deep. Where can you get this living water?" (John 4:11) He replies kind of cryptically, explaining that everyone who drinks that water (from the well) will be thirsty again—but those who drink the living water he offers will never thirst again.

If we fast forward through this recorded conversation, we find out that our sister has several failed relationships, although we don't know the reason. Jesus tries to tilt the conversation to the spiritual side, but she avoids answering any of his questions. Finally, she does her best to shut Jesus down: "When the Messiah comes, he's going to explain everything to us." Jesus says, "I, who you speak of, am He." (John 4:26)

Likely astounded, she ran back in town and told the other Samaritans that this man knew everything she ever did, and the verses that follow tell us many more people became believers in Jesus as the Messiah as a result.

Free Bird, here's what I want us to realize: Our Samaritan sister was ashamed and went to the well in the middle of the day, the hottest part of the day, because she could not travel with the other women. She went alone in the sweltering heat. I'm not her, so I can't be sure, but I can imagine that shame would be a driving force for her going alone. She wasn't welcomed in other circles because of her relational history, we do know that much. Where shame led her, Jesus met her. And the same thing is still true for us. Do you know what's super cool for us to note here? Jesus never suggests to her that getting married would be a solution to her problems and shame. Instead, He offers Himself as the solution. Come on now!

Marriage Culture in the Church

Our culture is obsessed with marriage. If you're a Christian, it is especially obsessive. There is a platform for married people and shame seats in the church for those of us who aren't. Do you think churches neglect Paul's call in the Scripture to serve rather than to simply get married to be married? What does the Bible say about marriage? Among other things, it says that God instituted marriage and gives it His blessing (Mark 10:6-9), that an ideal marriage relationship mirrors God's loving relationship with His people (Isaiah 62:5), and that a strong marriage relationship is a precious thing (Proverbs 31:10). Listen, marriage is a really good gift, but it is a terrible god, and for unmarried women in the church, it seems to be that the church often makes marriage a god. I think everyone is looking for a spot in the church, and there *is* a place for everyone. If you've participated in Christian education at a higher level at all, you've certainly heard about the "MRS" Degree, or the age-old adage, "Ring by spring or your money back!" or praying about the "one" God has for you. This rhetoric is hurtful and perpetuates the mistaken belief that marriage is the end goal instead of obedience to a God who loves us deeply.

Remember I told you I recently interviewed several women who are either currently unmarried or who got married later than the world was comfortable with? Well, when I asked, "How can the church do a better job at supporting unmarried women?" the responses from the majority of women were almost identical.

What do you think they said? How do you want to answer that question right now?

The overwhelming response was that the Christian church must change the narrative around being unmarried. While there was incredible agreement on marriage being an important covenant and institution of the church, the thoughts and feelings of many unmarried women were that they feel as though the church is imparting shame because they have yet to reach a goal the church has set *for* them. It seems to be that it feels like marriage is the goal of the church, but it shouldn't be. Love should always be our goal. So, is that where our shame comes from? Is shame something that we create for ourselves? Is it a result of others' expectations being unmet, is it shared, is it an embarrassment that we haven't met this life milestone yet? Who creates the milestones around here anyway? According to the survey, shame is imparted on us from others within the same church we love and serve. The church often talks about singleness as a season, but what if it's not a season? It is imperative that we carefully craft our words when speaking to each other. The women surveyed often discussed a disdain for how the church approaches conversations with single women, specifically.

Referring to someone's beautiful single life as a "season" often drove the cycle of shame with women who weren't sure they were going to be married in the first place. Why is someone's unmarried life referred to a season and someone's married life referred to as whole? That vocabulary induces shame. Do all you can to shake it, and be willing to have the difficult, corrective, loving conversations with those perpetuating the cycle.

What I think our sister from Samaria shows us is that shame will never take us anywhere that Jesus will not meet us. This is our battle cry, Free Bird. We are created for union with Him, and if God sees fit to give us a spouse, then that's a gift. But we are not wrong because we don't have one, and we are not diseased because we are unmarried. We are known by the Creator of the universe and called into freedom with Him. That freedom from shame is already available for you right now if you would claim it.

I've often found that the deep shame I have experienced is a result of someone else's feelings about my situation, stage of life, or thoughts. The look on my friend's faces when I tell them about another bad date or showing up to another family wedding without a plus one is something that is hard to shake. Often, we're taking on someone else's feelings about our own situation, instead of just operating in the freedom that we're called to. Isn't it interesting when we take on the feelings of others and put them on our own lives? How much freedom could we live in if we just owned it? Additionally, I'm wondering how many of us are dealing with the expectations we place on ourselves that don't come true? What happens when we don't meet our *own* expectations of how our lives turn out? Does this bring about shame for us as well?

The best thing we can do is partner with the church to be a part of the solution. Set up a time to meet with your pastor. Meet with the people who oversee women's ministry. Go meet with some friends where everyone in the circle cares about this same thing and start the ministry that you are searching for. I am sorry for our disappointment in the church, but a lot of people are disappointed in the church. Divorced people can be disappointed in the church. People of several different races can feel disappointed in the church they have experienced. People with small children can be disappointed in how the church is handling their children's ministry, and those with teenagers, student ministry. I feel disappointed about areas of the church, of course, but the solution is me. The solution is if you want to see something change in the community where you live, start being part of changing it. Our leaders cannot change the narrative, invest well in unmarried women, and respond to the need if they do not know the need exists. It is an unfair expectation of our church leaders. Go, sister! Be the change!

How can the church help the unmarried person thrive? Maybe the question should be: How can the church help everyone thrive regardless of relationship status, or occupation, or income? We have to start inviting people into the abundance that God has called each to by helping people find, experience, and encourage each other to operate in our respective gifting and calling, regardless of anything else. No matter our relationship status, it is the calling of the church to invest in the spiritual development of her people, not impart shame.

Guilty!

I think that shame has another lifelong friend in guilt. I was struggling with deep guilt one time and a precious mentor said something to me that I will never forget. "Guilt is not from God, Megan." She said, "Conviction is from the Holy Spirit and results in a change of behavior, but guilt—guilt is never something that God would want for His children. If you are convicted, then say you are sorry and change your way of living—but if you are guilty, let's figure out a way to shake that off." Friend, why is it that our shame and guilt go hand in hand?

Guilt is typically a feeling that arises when we think we have done something wrong. Shame is the feeling that our whole self is wrong.

Guilt says, "I did this wrong," and shame says, "I am wrong." Because our culture is obsessed with marriage, especially if you are a Christian, the very definitions of these feeling words give us insight into why we take them on as we do. As an unmarried woman in church culture, guilt says, "I haven't achieved this goal of marriage that other people have set before me." While in tandem, shame says, "I must be the problem; there must be something wrong with me because I am not married. I am wrong."

Everyone's favorite shame researcher, Brené Brown, says this in her article titled "Shame Vs. Guilt": "I define shame as the intensely painful feeling or experience of believing that we are flawed and therefore unworthy of love and belonging—something we've experienced, done, or failed to do makes us unworthy of connection. I don't believe shame is helpful or productive. In fact, I think shame is much more likely to be the source of destructive, hurtful behavior than the solution or cure. I think the fear of disconnection can make us dangerous."

The fear of disconnection, or the fear of not belonging, can make us dangerous to ourselves and to others in our sphere of influence. Spouses and children are incredible ways that people make connections in the world today, especially the Christian world. When we are walking into a church alone, there is not only a feeling of anxiety that can arise, but an incredible feeling of disconnectedness that already exists because we are alone in that place. What are unmarried women afraid of? Well, in the church culture I would say—being judged and having others pity us which perpetuates the cycle that we are not enough, that we have not arrived yet, and that we are incomplete until finding a spouse. Because of the disconnectedness, we make decisions and say things that our whole, healthy self would not decide or say. Maybe you've felt similarly before.

From the day we are born, we are learning if we are okay or not okay, accepted or unaccepted in the world that we live in. Our self-worth is created by our daily interactions as children whether we were praised and esteemed, or chastised and demeaned. We are learning who we are and what we mean and how we fit into the world by whether we are punished or disciplined, cared for or neglected. Feelings of shame are often projected feelings based on what other people think, not who we actually are.

Free Bird, let's recognize these feelings, but let's not live in them or operate out of them. If you are struggling with shame, guilt, or fear, I want to encourage you to seek the best therapy you can to understand their roots and how to live without them. Just like the woman at the well, they may take us somewhere we do not want to be, but Jesus will always meet us in that exact same place.

It is difficult to shake shame while guilt is demanding our attention. You tell guilt where to go and you get to the root of the shame. How? Well, that's between you and God. Therapy, prayer, small group, journaling, exercising—you tell me! What works for you?

After my initial healing and a few months of shame-shaking, I called my therapist one day in a full-blown panic. Now, I do not panic. I am not a panic girl. I was in a staff meeting at work and something someone said put me right back into the pit of shame. It was really disheartening, but I could not articulate exactly what was going on. So, I called Nonie. She answered and in her kind and loving way, asked questions to help me figure out what was really going on. Together, we determined the root of my feeling was shame. I cried harder at the realization. I felt sad that I was feeling shame. What a cycle! Choosing not to let shame drive that healing season was a harder decision than I anticipated. A daily, conscious choice was made each morning I opened my eyes, walked into work, the grocery store, or the gym. Shame was not in charge here, I was.

Do you feel shame because you are unmarried? Is there guilt associated with any life choices that led to where you are right now? You shake it right off. We are called to freedom living, not shameful living. These truths are bedrock to contentment, peace, joy, and being able to love authentically from a place of security in God's love. Single, dating, engaged, married, divorced, widowed—it can all well up certain similar feelings within us. Our insecurities follow us into every status and no relationship will ever remove the root of those anxieties and fears expect Jesus. He will always meet us.

Hang in there, Free Bird. It is about to get really good. You are carefully crafted in the image of God and have submitted your life to Jesus; therefore, you are already enough.

With you,
Megan

SHAME
CHECKLIST

◯ Read the story of the woman at the well in your favorite translation of the Bible. (John 4)

◯ In five minutes of complete silence, check in with yourself. Are you in a season of feeling shame, guilt, or fear? If so, write it out! If not, keep going, sister!

◯ Write a letter to someone forgiving them for a time when they placed their expectations and emotions unfairly on you. Rip up the letter.

◯ Watch Brené Brown's TEDTalk called "The Power of Vulnerability."

◯ Take a walk and drink some water.

CHAPTER 4

Owning It

PITFALL THINKING

If I fully embrace this, I will be labeled
as the single girl forever.

PURPOSE THINKING

Embracing where I am in life will
allow me to operate in total freedom
and in the fullness of surrender.

Hey Conqueror,

Are you familiar with the story in the Bible where Jesus calms a super big, scary storm? If you are or if you aren't, check it out:

> "That day when evening came, he said to his disciples, 'Let us go over to the other side.' Leaving the crowd behind, they took him along, just as he was, in the boat. There were also other boats with him. A furious squall came up, and the waves broke over the boat, so that it was nearly swamped. Jesus was in the stern, sleeping on a cushion. The disciples woke him and said to him, 'Teacher, don't you care if we drown?' He got up, rebuked the wind, and said to the waves, 'Quiet! Be still!' Then the wind died down and it was completely calm. He said to his disciples, 'Why are you so afraid? Do you still have no faith?' They were terrified and asked each other, 'Who is this? Even the wind and the waves obey him!'" Mark 4:35-41 NIV

Asleep. How could Jesus be asleep?

Seemingly terrified, his boys wake him up and ask if he even cares that they might die. Jesus wakes up, tells the wind and the waves to calm down, and then asks the disciples why they are so scared. Naturally, they're full of wonder—*or completely freaked out*, I'm not sure which.

I'm not sure if this is biblically accurate, so don't come for me—but I picture this whole interaction super casual. I envision Jesus—fully human, being awakened by chaos, groggy-eyed—and it's not this big, powerful "QUIET, BE STILL!" coming from His mouth, but rather a more casual . . . *"Can you not*?" to the wind and the waves.

I like to believe that He was completely unimpressed with this storm that was shaking the faith of the disciples. When the storm was raging and Jesus was sleeping, the disciples were all, *"You need to wake up to what is going on!"* Jesus gets up and is all, *"You need to wake up to who I am!"*

I wonder how many times we do the same—let Jesus know about the storms and chaos in our lives. I find an incredibly compelling truth in the story that follows this story. Can you hang around and hear me for one more minute? Check this out:

When Jesus and the disciples do finally arrive on the other side, they are immediately met by a man possessed by many demons. He was so strong that even chains could not hold him, and everyone was afraid to pass him by. This man was aggressive and violent. Not only that; he lived among these tombs, where many dead bodies were, and was therefore constantly in touch with death—the ultimate no-no in Jewish law. Both inside and out, this man was as corrupted as he could be—socially and otherwise.

Jesus approaches this man, the one no one else even comes close to approaching. He is no longer acting as casual as I picture him to be on the boat. Now we see Jesus relentlessly pursuing the demons that afflict this poor man's soul (Mark 5:8). Now, He is on the offensive.

Earlier, when Jesus says to his disciples, "Let us go over to the other side" (Mark 5:35), he is not just making a random suggestion. He moves with purpose, knowing that the other side of the lake is a battleground. He will confront the servants of his enemy, and he will be victorious. So, while they are crossing, no matter the strength of the wind or the size of the waves, Jesus is completely unconcerned. He already knows what lies ahead. He is not confronting the enemy in the storm; rather, the enemy lies on the other side of it. As it turns out, there is actually nothing to fear on the water.

Do not miss this: The storm is not the point.

They had to go through the storm to get to the other side, where the real purpose of the journey was.

Storms threaten to sink our faith. I'm not talking about everyday inconveniences like a flat tire, or something annoying at work. I'm talking about the difficulties that cause us to question God's goodness. Maybe it's an illness, the death of someone you love, a marriage yet to come to fruition, a marriage destroyed, financial hardship—and it feels like God is asleep. If He really cared, then maybe He'd stop this from happening, we might think. We pray for healing, for relief, for opportunity, for reconciliation, for anything that will make the storm pass. We may feel like our life as an unmarried person in today's culture is one intense storm that we are having to navigate seemingly alone. The bills? We've got them all. Car trouble? You know it. Big decision? All ours!

If we are going to own our purpose and walk in the abundance God has for us, we cannot be threatened by the storms that surround us, forgetting that Jesus is with us. It feels stormy when we don't get what we want, right? When our lives aren't turning out how we thought they should, it's easy to question purpose and calling surrounded by the storm—but it is easier to see it when we remember that Jesus is in the boat with us.

What we see in this story, however, is that the storm is not the whole point. The storm is real and terrifying—the disciples believe they will not survive—but the point is not about surviving the storm. The point is about Who is in the boat with them. Yes, Jesus can calm the storms in our lives. But Jesus did not come to calm us; He came to save us. Jesus did not come to give us a comfortable life; He came to defeat death.

I am not trying to diminish anyone's suffering, nor would I ever, ever, ever suggest that we cannot cry out to Jesus about the storms in our lives. He does, after all, get up and calm the storm in this story. And the Bible is full of encouragement to take our troubles to Him! I've suffered my fair share of storms and have sometimes cried out to Jesus and other times suffered alone.

It's not that Jesus doesn't care about our problems: He for sure does—A LOT. It's just that our problems aren't going to sink the boat while He's in it. What's on our list of problems as unmarried people in today's culture? The same problems everyone who is married has; only we deal with them alone.

Jesus fulfills His purpose in this stormy story to bring healing and restoration to the world. Do your current situations in life feel a little stormy to you? They do to me! What if your purpose was on the other side of this storm? The storm is where you meet your God.

Storms are frightening, I know. I know what it is to think I cannot survive or to think God doesn't care, or care enough, to do something about the pain the storm is causing. I know what it is to feel useless, helpless, and hopeless. And if that's how you are feeling right now, know that He knows. He is present with you and loves you.

But hear me clearly today: There is greater purpose on the other side of the storm.

I know there are a lot of people in chaos-like storms right now. You're likely navigating a life full of questions about the future: Will I have a job? What will my life look like if I don't get married? What is right? Is this really happening? How am I going to pay my bills? How am I going to do this alone? What is safe for me? What is right for me? How am I supposed to make this decision alone?

I suggest taking your eyes off the storm and focusing on Who is in the boat with you. Consider the greater purpose that waits on the other side of the storm.

If we're so hyper-focused on the storm and the chaos, we can't be focused on the Giver of Peace and the Calmer of Storms and the Fulfiller of all Purpose.

There are a lot of us walking around right now in absolute fear because of some of the hardships that come with unmarried life: fear of the storm, fear of the future, fear of the unknown, fear of the alone, fear of the consequence of a decision you need to make for your family, yourself, or those you love. My guess is if we can take our focus off the storm and the chaos and shift it to seeking the intended purpose on the other side of the storm—or better yet, Who is in our boat—our hearts, minds, and souls would be brought to a more peaceful place.

I was driving to the airport in the middle of the night. Truly, I left my home at 2:45 a.m. and began the hour drive to the closest airport. I was hardly awake but somehow had adrenaline—do you know the feeling that I'm talking about? It was November in the northeast, so it was dark—I'm talking, really dark. It was so incredibly dark that I could only see exactly what was right in front of me, the road, tree line, and other cars that were illuminated by my car's own headlights. I was starting to get nervous as tired and dark are two places where I do not generally thrive. In a moment of panic, I felt a peace come over me. *"You're seeing exactly what you need to see. The next part of the road ahead is all you need."* And that, Conqueror, is exactly what it takes to own this part of our lives. Contentment is trusting that we're seeing exactly what we need to see and that the next turn in the road ahead is all we need to keep driving on the right road.

Where do you need to create a shift today?

We create shifts by transforming our thinking away from the chaos of our pitfalls and onto our purpose.

If the disciples could see the purpose on the other side of the storm, my guess is that they wouldn't have freaked out in the middle of it.

Where do you need to make a conscious, waking choice, to see past the storm and into purpose? Peace, be still. He is with you!

How do we do it? Let's figure it out together. Embracing the season will allow you to operate in total freedom and in the fullness of surrender.

Surrendered,
Megan

OWNING IT
CHECKLIST

◯ Think about, write about, and talk about a time when your life was a little stormy.

◯ Write about a time when you felt like your boat was sinking. If it is right now, know that you are seen, heard, and known.

◯ Consider: What might be the purpose awaiting you on the other side of your storm?

◯ Own something this week! Walk into that room, send that email, call that guy, schedule that appointment, reach that goal!

◯ Take a walk and drink some water.

CHAPTER 5

Family Ties

PITFALL THINKING

Because I do not have a husband
or children of my own, I do not add
value to my family structure.

PURPOSE THINKING

I have purpose no matter where I am.

"Then Jesus' mother and brothers arrived. Standing outside, they sent someone in to call him. A crowd was sitting around him, and they told him, 'Your mother and brothers are outside looking for you.' 'Who are my mother and my brothers?' he asked. Then he looked at those seated in a circle around him and said, 'Here are my mother and my brothers! Whoever does God's will is my brother and sister and mother.'" Mark 3:31-34 NIV

Hey Sister,

Remember our conversation about being a little girl? Well, that's where it all begins. We are someone's little girl. It doesn't matter if we come from a two-parent home, a one-parent home, or a foster home; all our longings begin when we're children. (That's what the experts tell us anyway!) Because of life's circumstances, some may long for more than others, or less than others, but the longing exists, nonetheless. What longing, you ask? Well, I'd venture to say most of them: the longing for acceptance, the longing for family, the longing for dependability, the longing for value and worth, and the longing for a peaceful soul. All because we've been brought into this world, we're somebody's someone longing for something.

I love being somebody's someone. In fact, I wish I was more people's someone. Specifically, one person's someone. My longing is to feel the peace of being chosen. The peace of knowing that someone chose me to be their someone. So how do I navigate not being someone's someone in a family surrounded by everyone's someones? Maybe you feel similar. Here's what I know, and what we can do together.

A few weeks before my older brother got married, several members of our extended family were out to dinner together at a local restaurant.

Our younger brother graduated high school that year, I had my first article published that year, and our older brother was getting married! What a year for the Faulkner kids.

When someone at dinner brought that up, someone else said, "Just for the record, he wins!" pointing toward my older brother.

"Why does he win?" I asked, feeling incredibly accomplished at having a writing dream come true.

"He's getting married!" came the response. Ouch.

Marriage was always a dream of mine, or better yet, a goal, but I didn't realize I wouldn't "win" in my own family until that was accomplished. My family was proud of me; my parents made a big deal about my publishing, and they even bought me some artwork for my wall to celebrate. It was so kind and thoughtful, and it meant a lot to me. But I did not *win*. Those words echoed through my soul for many years, feeling like I truly would not be accomplished until I had a husband of my own.

So how do we navigate life unattached in family gatherings, on family vacations, and in settings where the value of family is highly esteemed, specifically? I, too, have a high regard for family. I place high value on my familial relationships, our time together, and who I am in those settings. Navigating life unmarried to this point, I decided one thing was for certain: I would unapologetically be myself. There are two things that are non-negotiables for me: cultivating relationships within my family, and showing up. Regardless of marital status, those two things are absolutely possible in whatever situation we find ourselves in. While our families may place a high value on marriage, and we might too, we can navigate family gatherings beautifully in the meantime.

These years are like little gifts given to us, tied in a really ugly bow and placed in our hands. Sometimes it feels like everyone is watching us open them, unsure of what's in the box. But the gift of time can't be lost on us. It may not be the gift we want, but it is the gift we've been given right now. So, the question becomes: How do we use it well?

Cultivating relationships within the family is one of the greatest gifts we can give to others.

Let me take a pause right here to say something that may be important for some to read: If your family isn't safe, go ahead and skip this part. There are a lot of women who are navigating unsafe family situations full of abuse and hardship as a result of someone else's choices. I would never suggest cultivating a relationship with an abuser. This isn't for you. But, sweet sister, I want you to know that you are seen, heard, and known. Your family can be the family of your choosing: the family God has provided for you through incredible friends, neighbors, small groups, or church. Maybe your family are the people you spend time with at work, or at your gym, or participating in whatever community event or hobby brings you a lot of joy. Family doesn't always mean blood relations. In fact, check out the Scripture at the top of the chapter. For Jesus, anyone doing the will of God was family. The bottom line is that if it is unsafe for you to cultivate relationships within your blood family, do it within your chosen family. You'll love the results.

Okay, back to relationship cultivation! I have a friend who asks excellent questions. She will walk into a room, find someone, and start asking questions about their life, their work, their beliefs, their dreams, goals, and desires. It is remarkable. Some of our friends tell her that she is too intrusive, but I think it's hilarious. Do you know what she knows about people? Almost everything! People love answering her questions. How do we cultivate great relationships? We ask great questions! I'm nowhere near as good at this as my friend, but I've discovered the power in asking questions. People just want to be seen, heard, and known—even people in our own families! It may seem like we know everything there is to know about our family already, but I'd push back and say that's not true especially if we don't live with or near them. My dad and brothers are always working on new projects at work. My sisters-in-law know all the cutest details of my nieces' and nephews' lives that I don't get to see because I'm not there. My mom has so many people in her life; there is always something new and interesting going on in her world! So, if I want to know, I must ask questions.

Cultivating a relationship isn't all about asking and answering questions. We know this. It's being there for the good moments and the bad. It's having the easy conversations and the difficult ones. It's proving that you can be trusted and having others earn your trust as well. It's walking through fire with your family and coming out on the other side.

Extended family gatherings always feel tricky to me, not because anyone makes them feel that way, but because *I* feel a certain way about them. When cousins younger than me started getting engaged, married, and having babies, an insane jealousy bubbled up inside of me, and sometimes it flowed straight out of my eyeballs. My mom would call with the news, "So-and-so is pregnant!" and I felt like I wanted to crawl in a cave and stay there for the remainder of time. But what is a good friend to do? No matter how I felt about any of it, I had to show up.

Decide how you want to show up: Will you bring the fun? Will you have deep meaningful conversations? Will you make the plan and stick to it? Who will you be when it's just you and seven married couples sitting around a table for a backyard barbecue to celebrate your niece's first birthday?

Do you want to hear the good news? You get to decide. If we live with a heart full of resentments and frustration, we will show up resentful and frustrated. If we live with a heart full of peace and seeking purpose, we will show up peaceful and purposeful. No one else gets to dictate how you show up in these settings. As unmarried women, we can show up with fun and purpose, in love and with peace. I personally show up with charcuterie, because who doesn't love cheese and meat on a wooden board? It's incredible how often showing up with something in your hand breaks the ice. Suddenly, people who have big feelings about your marital status will lose focus on what you don't have and begin focusing on what you do have! (*See me for more party tips and tricks.*)

CHAPTER 5 - FAMILY TIES

Truthfully, showing up is half the battle. Do you feel similar? It's often hard to convince myself that I will be okay in a family setting full of married people and babies. It feels like everyone is on the same page and I am left behind. But again, that's my choice. I can choose to approach the family gathering like that, or I can choose to approach it with fun and compassion and with a heart seeking connection and joy.

If you're not sure where to start, what about inviting your family into your space? Host your family for the weekend or invite them over for dinner if you're close enough in distance. Or dare I suggest, host Thanksgiving! *(All the aunties gasp!)* Show them what you're made of, girl! You are strong and you are capable, and you can entertain regardless of whether you have the right measuring cups from Anthropologie. I have an unmarried friend who is in her fifties. Girlfriend loves her life and hosts all the time. She is an excellent cook, her family begs to spend time with her, and she is the woman with the plan! She's an excellent relationship cultivator, shows up for her family all the time, and hosts them constantly. Everyone loves going to her house. I'm not sure it's because her food is so good, although it is; I think it's because she makes everyone feel seen and known and heard. She asks great questions, has great ideas, is always looking for fun, and makes everyone who walks through her doors feel so special.

What gifts do you possess that would make showing up to a family gathering or hosting one in your own space a success? Are you funny, fun, and the life of the party? Be that, party girl! Do you have excellent ideas and want to host? Send out those invites! Are you the best Auntie in the world? Invite those nieces and nephews over for a day of fun with you. Marriage is not the stamp of approval dictating when you can or cannot be full of life and fun. Married people do not get to host just because they are married. Set a new path, forge a way, and start inviting! Maybe you do this already—good for you! I'm proud. Host the holidays that others deem untouchable, bring the best desserts, and be the most fun. Truthfully, I have a lot of disdain for the *Crazy Aunt* stamp that the world uses to place on unmarried women, but sister, be crazy! You are calling all your own shots right now. Do not miss the chance! You might not have these days forever.

Family relationships can be difficult to navigate because that seems to be the place where people feel the most freedom to ask about your life. It's perfectly acceptable for you to want to set boundaries around which conversations are appropriate and inappropriate to have in a family setting. Not everyone gets access to all of you. What we are called to do, as Christians, is to navigate those conversations with grace and compassion. Setting an example in our families, even to generations before us, may be a challenging task, but Sister, we have accomplished more difficult things. If you are not interested in talking about your dating life, you don't have to. If you are interested in talking about your dating life, bring it up! If you're not interested in talking about work, say you would like to enjoy the family day and change the subject. These things seem simple, but sometimes we must give each other permission to just be. What you think is valid and who you are in your family matters. Choose how you will respond and be unapologetically yourself. That's all our family wants anyway—just us!

Whatever it looks like, whatever you have—invite your family into it. You don't need someone else, and you don't need to be someone else. Just be you. You are the right one to do it. You have purpose, no matter where you are.

With you,
Megan

FAMILY TIES
CHECKLIST

◇ Check in with yourself the next time you are about to go to a family gathering. How do you feel? Do you need to do any heart prep before you go?

◇ Pick something to bring with you! Bubbles for the kids? Charcuterie?

◇ Show up.

◇ Write down five good questions for family members that you hope to know the answers to at the end of your family gathering.

◇ Take a walk and drink some water.

CHAPTER 6

FWB: Friends with Babies

PITFALL THINKING

My friends are seen as more mature than I am because
they have babies and I do not.

PURPOSE THINKING

Being a wife or mother does not make someone more
or less mature. Because I am pursuing His plan for my life,
I am mature and complete in Christ, lacking nothing.

"As the Father has loved me, so have I loved you. Now remain in my love. If you keep my commands, you will remain in my love, just as I have kept my Father's commands and remain in his love. I have told you this so that my joy may be in you and that your joy may be complete. My command is this: Love each other as I have loved you. Greater love has no one than this: to lay down one's life for one's friends." John 15:9-13 NIV

Hey Auntie,

"*Megan.*" My friend's voice was serious on the phone that day. "There is no shortcut to maturity. Motherhood and wifehood do not make you mature. We are all being made mature every day." I knew she meant the truth she was sharing, and it brought me to tears.

Rewind about seven years.

"You wouldn't understand; you don't have a child." The words stung deep into my core.

The person speaking to me was right; I didn't know what it was like to have a biological child. I do, however, know what it's like to love another tiny human so much that the very thought of it brings tears to my eyes. I know what it's like to worry about education, health care, and social skills. I've wondered about where they fit in, who their friends are, and if they feel safe.

I don't know what it's like to buy diapers or to breastfeed, but I know how to shake up formula, and I've watched my fair share of little bestie temper tantrums in the middle of the frozen foods aisle of the grocery store.

I do know what it's like to buy a new backpack, purchase school supplies, buy shoes, new t-shirts, school registrations, and the occasional puzzle or book, but she was right—I didn't know what it was like to be the sole provider for another human.

And what she didn't know is my heart shattered into 45 million little pieces that day, just like that vase the day when I became unstuck.

Other Mothering Moments

A beautiful twenty-one-year-old young woman sat on the couch in my home on a sizzling summer day. It was June, and her precious mom had passed away from cancer just a month prior. I asked her if she wanted to come over that day to talk, and she replied with a joyful, yet somewhat relieved, "Yes, please."

We sat on my couch talking about the current affairs of the world, when I looked at her and said "Hey, how are you really?" She replied, "I'm glad you asked me to come over; I was wondering if we could talk about some things. I have some questions." *Enter true panic here.* This sweet love just lost her precious mama about thirty days prior, and I worried she had some big questions that I did not have big answers to. I took a deep breath and said, "Sure, honey, what's on your mind?"

"Well," she said, "I have a bridal shower next weekend and I just have some questions. I would normally ask my mom, but . . ." and her voice tapered off as her eyes filled up.

"What are your questions?" I asked.

"Okay, so, I bought something off the registry and sent it to their house. Do I need to bring a gift to the shower as well?"

"Oh no, sweetheart, that is the gift. Just take a card with you and write a little note in it to them saying you hope they like it. Maybe provide the receipt if you're able."

"Okay, I'll do that," she calmly said. "But Megan . . . "

"Yeah?"

"I don't know what to wear. I'm a bridesmaid. I also don't really know what to do, or what my roles are, or what I'm supposed to take. I didn't get to this part of life with my mom yet, I don't know what to do, and my dad, he's so great but he is no help. Can I just ask you questions about all of this?"

CHAPTER 6 - FWB: FRIENDS WITH BABIES

My eyes filled with tears. She did not get to have this conversation with her mom, so she had it with *me*. I was heartbroken and my heart was swelling, I was so sad, and so grateful she thought she could come to me to ask.

We spent the next hour discussing all of the details of being a bridesmaid, the expectations, the what to wear when, when to show up, how to show up well, what to do to actually help, when to bring champagne, when to bring a gift, how to not be in the way and be present, what gifts are appropriate when, and how to stand by your friend while she's taking these vows. I've done this job nineteen times—I wish I were lying to you—so I had a lot of answers for this love bug on a Wednesday afternoon in June.

I did not deserve to have this conversation with her. Her mom did. Her mom had lost a baby prior to my young friend and her brother's birth, twins, whom their mom had always deemed a double blessing. She had fought for her babies, waited so long for them—talk about a woman who knew how to wait well! I did not deserve to have the bridesmaid discussion. But I was the one who got to have it—and what a privilege it was.

So, you are right. I do not know what it's like to have children. But I do know what it's like to help support a few, and I hope I'm doing it justice.

What Do We Do?

But what happens when all our friends start having babies and we're still on dating apps swiping left, presumably, because there are just no men left out there in the world? First, we cry. Second, we just have to handle it.

It's fun when our first friends start having our little besties. We get to be the Auntie and then we get to go home and sleep cozy in our beds uninterrupted for a full night's sleep. That is not the case for our new mommy friends. The grass always feels greener, doesn't it?

While this sounds absolutely wild to the people in our lives who are married and have kids, this particular season of our lives is full

57

of sacrifice. I know that and you know that. But, what if we stopped thinking about our sacrifices and started thinking about our response? Everyone, regardless of marital status, spends a lot of their life giving a lot of themselves. Our time, our money, our love, and our energy get used on our families, our friends, our bosses, and our communities. We have a choice in how we are responding as unmarried women with no children in these situations. If we think of what we are doing—how we are showing up for our friends with babies, how we are spending time, effort, and money—as a sacrifice, then it will always, or maybe likely, have a negative connotation. I would like to challenge us as unmarried women with no children to be intentional in framing our internal thought process from sacrifice to service. I know we will find joy there.

If I could guess, I would venture to say what we all want while navigating these situations is to be seen and to continue to play a role in our friends' lives. Our friends with babies are seen, too. I'm not suggesting we unsee one just to see the other; I'm simply suggesting that we choose to see everyone. It's so much better if we're all seen.

Is it upsetting you that your friends are having babies and they don't ask you about your dating life? Well, then maybe consider saying to them, *"Hey, I wish you'd asked me more about my dating life"*. This will take a deep dive heart check to figure out, but are you upset with the simple fact that they're having babies and you're not? If so, I hate to be the one to break this news to you, but that is a jealousy thing. If it is a jealousy thing, then there's repentance and you need to turn from it, celebrating that God is giving them God's gifts for *them*.

No one is birthing a child you were meant to birth. God is Sovereign and His plan for your life is the most perfect one for *your* life. There is no gray area to the Sovereignty of God. So you can, in your pain and sadness (I'm not saying you need to pretend, but if jealousy is hurting a relationship . . .), have a conversation and fix it. If they truly are your actual friends, then you can tell them that you miss them asking about things that are happening in your life. It's okay. You are allowed to mourn what once was. God is not messing up your story and getting someone else's right.

How do we see our friends with babies? The same way we see our family. We actively choose to cultivate deep relationships and we show up. Our friends simply cannot always show up in the ways we need in this season of their lives, and that's okay; it's just our turn to show up right now.

It's pretty simple to show up for our friends in their baby years. Don't overthink it, Auntie. Drop off coffee, bring the bagels, stock the freezer full of ready-to-eat dinners, send fruit baskets and flowers, and be willing to participate in family life when you are around. Mom's changing the baby? No problem, you can start heating up lunch! Mom's laying the baby down for a nap? You've got the skills to help straighten up the living room in the meantime. It will mean the world to her.

I think what I am suggesting most in this season is that we show up with the same compassion we would like to receive. Would we like to be seen? Then let's see our friends. Would we like to be known? Then let's get to know what this season of their life is genuinely like. Would we like to be loved? Then let's love outrageously and with reckless abandon. Our friends need us, and they need us to still be their friends.

My mom friends have shared many times over the years that it is so easy to get stuck in their day-to-day child rearing that they often forget that a life exists outside of the walls of their house. They are so focused on the next feeding or changing that they struggle to maintain any life outside of what, or should I say, *who* is in front of them.

As aunties, we have the best role! We can still share life with our friends who are in different seasons than us. We can show up, chat, and remind our friends why we love them. We have the privilege of being a friend to a woman who sometimes needs to be reminded she is more than a milk machine, changing station, or laundromat. What an honor to serve as the role of rememberer for someone in their life. Reminisce with her, choose to remind her that she has a role in your life, too, and you in hers. In a podcast interview with shame researcher, Brené Brown, Holocaust survivor Dr. Edith Eger says "love is a four-letter word spelled t-i-m-e." How beautiful! We can love our friends in this season simply by sharing our t-i-m-e.

We do not lose our friends because they have children now; in fact, we need each other more than ever in this season. We, unmarried women, need to be reminded that there is hope for our futures and that we have roles to play in the lives of our little besties, and the women with babies need to be reminded that they are still fun and have purpose and have a calling in this wild life more than any of us could imagine.

How this season of life affects us is up to us. (Child-rearing years *are* a season, unmarried years may not be.) We can choose to see it through the lens of joy, excitement, and service, or we can choose to see it through the lens of resentment and frustration, digging our heels into all the changes around us.

Sure, there are times that our hearts will break. There are baby showers we will attend that we will barely get through if our desire is to have a family of our own and we cannot even get a second date. I have cried in the bathroom of more baby showers than I can even remember! There will be baptisms and first birthday parties that will feel a little bit like getting stung by a few bees at a time because we do not have these experiences of our own yet. But do you know what our friends are doing? They are inviting us into their lives. If you get the invitation to the party, show up. It may make your stomach wrap into 7,000 knots while you are walking in without your own kid, and you may feel a little out of place while everyone else is having kid conversations, so use that opportunity to serve. If we can see outside of ourselves, I think we can ask God to heal our wounds and be the best aunties to our little besties that we can be.

Maturity does not come from achieving life milestones set forth for us by society, and that is the tricky part. Some young married women often respond to their unmarried friends as though they have a leg up, or knowledge that the other has not attained yet. That thinking is dangerous and detrimental to relationships. Marital status and motherhood do not make us mature and complete; Jesus alone does, and He does not need the help of another.

You are mature and complete in Christ, lacking nothing.

Still here,
Megan

FRIENDS WITH BABIES CHECKLIST

⬡ Call a friend with a kid and ask to come over to hang out.

⬡ Pick something to bring with you! Books for the kids? Wine for your friend?

⬡ Help around her house.

⬡ Remind your friend that she is important as a person, not just because she is a mom.

⬡ Take a walk and drink some water.

CHAPTER 7

Dating: Persistent Widow Vibes

PITFALL THINKING

I need to have the most exciting dating life;
but there is just no one to date!

PURPOSE THINKING

I will trust in God with all my heart and
follow Him wherever He leads me.

"Then Jesus told his disciples a parable to show them that they should always pray and not give up. He said: 'In a certain town there was a judge who neither feared God nor cared what people thought. And there was a widow in that town who kept coming to him with the plea, 'Grant me justice against my adversary.' For some time, he refused. But finally, he said to himself, 'Even though I don't fear God or care what people think, yet because this widow keeps bothering me, I will see that she gets justice, so that she won't eventually come and attack me!' And the Lord said, 'Listen to what the unjust judge says. And will not God bring about justice for his chosen ones, who cry out to him day and night? Will he keep putting them off? I tell you, he will see that they get justice, and quickly. However, when the Son of Man comes, will he find faith on the earth?'" Luke 18:1–8 NIV

Hey Love,

I often feel like the persistent widow in the gospels and I'm wondering if you do, too? There are years and years of journals that are filled with the same unanswered prayers. Well, seemingly unanswered anyway. I've been asking God for a husband for longer than I can remember, and here I am, writing a book about being unmarried in today's culture. This is not how I thought it would all play out. Does your life look a little different from what you imagined at this point, too? Are you tired of swiping left or having first dates that make you feel like you're on a hidden camera TV show? Or maybe you're tired of having no dates at all. Girlfriend, you are not alone in any of those situations. Maybe dating isn't something that you're interested in at all, and we'll address that in a little bit, so if that's you—hang tight.

But, if we want a relationship, where do we go to find it?

Love, I am so glad you asked because I have been wondering about the same thing for thirty-something years! My friends have been meeting the men of their dreams and I can't seem to make it past a few months in a relationship with a man before he ruins it. *(Obviously nothing is ever my fault, right?)*

Before we can even consider looking for authentic companionship, I want to bring something to the forefront that may seem controversial for some of us. Have you been to therapy? I don't mean you've had one session of online therapy and called it a day—I mean, have you forged a relationship with a licensed therapist and done the hard work of learning and unlearning all the things you need to learn and unlearn? I am not for one second suggesting that something is wrong with you and that's why you're not dating, I'm suggesting that we offer the very best of ourselves to the entire world regardless of if we're dating or not. One way to get there is through a safe, comfortable, and hard-working relationship with a licensed therapist. Why not give our full selves to a broken, hurting, and needy world that so desperately needs to encounter love? We have it to give! One of the best investments of my entire life has been my sweet therapist. She had to do some digging, but a few sessions in, I was finally able to discover that I felt an incredible amount of shame that I was thirty-something and unmarried.

She didn't scoff at me, or say that my shame was ridiculous, she asked, *"Why do you think you feel shame?"* I couldn't get to that point yet, but I was desperately trying to and really wanted to.

She shared something true I hadn't heard said aloud to me before: *"Megan,"* she looked right at me, *"If you wanted to be married to someone, you could be. But you are not looking for just someone. You are looking for someone awfully specific. Keep looking for him. You could leave my office today and find someone to marry! But I'm not sure that's the best route for you. You know who you are looking for, and that's okay."* Imagine how freeing that sounded, coming from a place of stuck and shame.

So, friend, if you're wanting to be married but are not yet, hear this same truth that was shared with me: If you wanted to be married to just anyone, you could be. But you are not looking for just anyone. You are looking for someone awfully specific.

And that is okay.

So how do we conduct ourselves while we're looking, and what does it look like to date while everyone else is already buying their second home and having their fifth baby? Well, let me tell you. It is equally all things awful and all things fun at the exact same time.

Single and Loving It?

Before we address dating in our marriage-obsessed culture, let me try to navigate one thing for us to think about together. I'm just not sold on the idea that everyone wants to date or even be married. Maybe you don't. Maybe you're uninterested in the things of dating. Sweet friend, hear this: That is a-okay. Just because the world says you should do something does not mean you have to do that. *All things are permissible,* the writer of Corinthians says, *but not all things are beneficial.* You could be living this beautiful part of your life where, sure, the world says it's acceptable for you to be dating and interested in the things of marriage, but if you are not, don't date just because someone says you should be dating. Save yourself the heartstring ties, the awful first dates, and the uncomfortable conversations. You're allowed to not want to date. Not that you need my permission to remain unmarried—you for sure do not—but I find it alarming that when women particularly are uninterested in dating, the world decides that something is terribly wrong.

Nothing is wrong with you! If you're uninterested, you're uninterested! You do you, girl. I have a friend who is unmarried and in her thirties who is very uninterested in dating and marriage. Whenever it is brought up, she quickly shuts it down. She knows her calling and is operating in it to the fullest. She is committed to the mission of her church, serves on a few different ministry teams, and loves her family very well. She has stated that dating and marriage are just not for her, that she's content and happy to serve how she's serving and live how she's living. Good for her, right? She's awesome. We need more of her in the world—women who are so certain of their purpose and calling. It's so beautiful!

Ready to Mingle?

There are those of us who are interested in dating and it just does not seem to be working out. There seems to be a deep longing inside us, and I believe we can walk ourselves through some reassuring sentiments that will allow us to pursue healthy dating boundaries and relationships.

How do we do it?

Let's be ourselves! Let's agree that we refuse to settle for false companionship. We are not the kind of women who are interested in settling. We are the kind of women who are interested in the real thing—the real, authentic, vulnerable, messy, compatible thing. We are not the fairytale girls who hold out for an unrealistic idea, and we are not the ones who don't believe in love, either—we are just not interested in companionship that isn't tangible.

False companionship does not just refer to settling; it could also mean that we are putting on a front and not being the best version of ourselves. Choose to be the best version of yourself, the one with the most authenticity. When you're in a space to meet new people, just be yourself. The world doesn't need anybody else again; the world just simply needs you. While there may be lies floating around the universe about how we're supposed to behave and what we're supposed to look like to gain companionship that's long-lasting, I would like to squash those lies right now. The only thing you need to be is you.

Settling should not be on our agenda. Imagine settling for companionship with someone who is not fully pursuing God like you are? Or someone whose core values don't align with your core values? Imagine being on a mission that is yours alone for the rest of your life while having someone you love question and belittle that mission? Love, we are not called to settle. It's okay to know what you want, it's okay to know who you want, and it's also okay to compromise on the things that are negotiable, but not the non-negotiable. Decide who you are looking for and what kind of companionship you desire. (This translates to all parts of life, not just dating! If we are going to be women of purpose and pursuit, these truths translate to careers, finances, communities, and the like! Don't compromise on the non-negotiables.)

I worked with an awesome youth worker one time who was talking to a group of girls in high school about their dating lives and the expectations around dating as Christians. She explained to them that dating is like shopping for a prom dress. Imagine the glow in these girls' eyes as they hear their youth worker compare dating to prom dress shopping! When you go shopping for a prom dress, she explained, your intent is to find the best dress with the right fit and the one that just stands out to you the most, the one you feel like your best self in, the one you feel most comfortable in, the one that makes you shine. The purpose of a prom dress is to wear the dress to prom. When you're at the prom dress store, you may try on a few dresses to see which one you like the best. But you're not going to the prom dress store to try on a pair of socks, you're going to the prom dress store to try on dresses you will hopefully love and purchase. The starry-eyed teenagers started to understand what she was saying.

Maybe you'll date one man, maybe you will date two or three or ten or fifteen, but ultimately the goal is to find the one that fits the best and makes you feel like your best self. You are out there looking for the best prom dress possible. You are not going prom-dress shopping and trying on socks. (And if you are, that's okay! Socks aren't bad. They just don't serve the same *purpose* as a prom dress!)

I'm not saying you need to make a list of demands for a relationship; in fact, I think that would be dangerous. What I am suggesting is that you take some time to consider exactly who you are looking for before you start looking for him. What kind of character do you want someone you're interested in to have? What kind of mission is he on, and does that match yours? Maybe it will take us a total of five minutes to decide who it is that you're interested in seeking, maybe it will take you five years, but wisdom says to think it through, so I think that's what you do. What kind of person do you want to be on mission with? Dating isn't always exciting; in fact, it's often pretty difficult. I have a few friends who are yet to be married, and if I could print the pages of the group chat about the dates we've been on, you would laugh and cry. Although if you're reading this book, I'm sure that you have done those things on your own already.

I don't necessarily subscribe to the notion that there is one right way to date and a wrong way to date. I think that if the cross is personal (and it is!) then our whole lives are personal. I will say, however, that in my experience, my dating relationships have been a reflection of my relationship with Jesus. What do I mean by that? If I am seeking God's will and heart for my life, I want to date, but a good or bad date doesn't make or break my week. If I'm not in a positive place with Jesus, a good or bad date seems to set the tone for how I respond to the things that are happening in the world around me. Are you the same?

Love, just take it all to Jesus. The good, the bad, the ugly, the right, the wrong, the hurt, the pain, the frustration, the excitement—there is nothing we experience that He alone can't handle. He is ready and willing and wants to hear from you. He is desiring a relationship with you that is beyond your wildest imagination and He will never stop pursuing you. I am certainly not one of those Christian girls who walks around saying, "I'm dating Jesus." I'm not dating Him; He is my Savior and so much more than any date! I am suggesting, however, that our relationship with Him matters more than any earthly relationship. Whether you are single, married, dating, engaged, or enraged, He is the one Truth that will never lie, fail, cheat, or steal your joy.

Ultimately, the choice to date is yours alone with your personal Savior. The choice to pursue a relationship further is yours alone with your personal Savior. The choice to maintain a relationship is yours alone with your personal Savior. But friend, it's all that: a choice. There is no obligation to this part of life. There are no mandatory expectations except to keep Jesus in it and ask Him for help in discerning the most abundant decision for your life. The gospel writer in John 10:10 tells us Jesus came so that we could have life and have it abundantly. That abundance isn't just about one thing—and abundance doesn't only come when we are married with children. You can have an abundant life now, in every situation. You can live well now, regardless of whether your Friday night calendar has a date written on it or not. You are created for abundance, and no relationship qualifies or disqualifies you.

I want you to know this: I know that it can get ugly. I know that comparing our dating lives to even our other unmarried friends' dating lives can put us right in the pit. Dating is difficult, at best. It is one of my least favorite things to do. It often exhausts me. Because I do want to be married, I feel like I must go on dates. But friend, if you are exhausted, tired, and worn down by dating, you are not alone. If you simply cannot find someone that you feel would be a good match, you are not obligated to go out on the date! Again, I know you are not looking for permission, but occasionally, we do need the validation. The comparison trap here is that the world makes it seem like everyone has these really Instagrammable dates, but that's not true.

Often, my married friends will tell me to "put myself out there." Out where?! What does that even mean? This unsolicited advice comes from friends who are incredibly well meaning but they married very young and have no idea what it is like to date through your twenties, thirties, and beyond. Isn't it funny? I love their advice about the things they are experts in, such as business endeavors, home purchasing, or whatever they are good at—but not dating! How fun is it to be told: *relax and it will happen.* That is by far my absolute favorite. (That was sarcasm, in case it didn't translate.) What's yours?

About the Persistent Widow

The very nature of the Persistent Widow reveals to us that faith is continuous. We can gather that maybe we should always pray, just like her, and not lose heart. Jesus uses this parable to teach his disciples to never give up. Jesus knows that life here on earth involves disappointment, loss, some forms of injustice, and many other reasons to give up hope. Perhaps you've given up hope in the dating world—it's easy to do! But a life in tune with God's presence, a life that is filled with purpose regardless of circumstance, a life seeking justice, is a life that can endure.

Is being unmarried an injustice of the world? I don't think so. Can it feel like that sometimes? Absolutely! Our thinking needs to shift from pitfall to purpose in order to see that we can be persistent in our attempts to connect with God, and therefore, never give up hope that His plans for us are best.

The paths God has for us have not always led where we thought they would, or where we've wanted them to. It is a waking, conscious choice for us to trust in Him in this dating season of life. It is not always beautiful, and it does not always look like shooting stars and smell like roses. This dating season often feels muddy, messy, and sometimes, even mean. You're not alone.

This difficult dating world is yours for the taking. The good news is that you get to decide your response. If you trust in God with all your heart, lean not on your own understanding, and in all your ways acknowledge Him, He will make your paths straight—no matter where they lead, even if it's to somewhere you do not want to be.

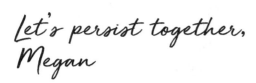

Let's persist together,
Megan

DATING CHECKLIST

⬡ Decide if dating is even something you are interested in right now.

⬡ Make a list, mental or otherwise, of the top non-negotiables in someone you would like to date.

⬡ Bring a friend into it! You are not alone. Share a dating fear with a trusted confidant.

⬡ Write down three good questions that you hope to know the answers to at the end of your date.

⬡ Take a walk and drink some water alone—or maybe not.

CHAPTER 8

Created for Community

PITFALL THINKING
Alone means lonely.

PURPOSE THINKING
I am created to live and participate
in thriving relationships with others.

Hey Friend,

The writer of Hebrews in the Bible knew that Jesus's followers would find incredible power in His sacrifice. His sacrifice, His death by crucifixion on the cross, has the power to change us—for eternity. And while that's helpful for the forever, we still live in the here and now. So, what do we do? Check this out from Hebrews 10:

> "Since we have a great priest over the house of God, let us draw near to God with a sincere heart and with the full assurance that faith brings, having our hearts sprinkled to cleanse us from a guilty conscience and having our bodies washed with pure water. Let us hold unswervingly to the hope we profess, for he who promised is faithful. And let us consider how we may spur one another on toward love and good deeds, not giving up meeting together, as some are in the habit of doing, but encouraging one another—and all the more as you see the Day approaching." Hebrews 10:21-25 NIV

There's an encouragement here for us as believers to continue living life together, holding onto hope, remembering the faithfulness of God, and encouraging one another to live a life of love and good deeds.

Unmarried days can be lonely days. An unmarried friend was struggling with some things in her workplace. We were together at another friend's house one night talking about the difficulties of a stressful work life. Listening to her speak, I realized that she hadn't told anyone any of her struggles for weeks, maybe even months.

"Hey," I said, "do you think it's a little bit harder sometimes because we have no one to come home and decompress with? No one to vent to?"

"Oh," she replied. "I never thought about that. But I think you're right. I just want to come home and go through the day with someone, but no one is there. I don't journal, maybe I should, and I don't call anyone, I just kind of sit there at the end of the day hoping maybe it will debrief itself."

We all laughed at the thought of the day debriefing itself, and because two of the three of us were unmarried, we also laughed at the sting. Sometimes it's easier to laugh about it all than it is to cry.

Not only did the Creator of the Universe design us; He designed us specifically to be together. When we're unmarried, community feels like something we must work a little harder at having because it's not naturally built into the fabric of our day. If we don't seek it out, create it, or nurture it, some days could be spent entirely alone. The pitfalls can get ugly for that reason.

Maybe you have an awesome group of friends, but maybe you don't. Maybe you're struggling and feeling lonelier than ever. There have been seasons of my life where friends were the highest priority. A lot of time was spent cultivating friendships and building fun weekends, and yet, some of those have also been times when I have felt the loneliest. Why? Well, I'm not sure I was my most true, authentic self. Letting others in on what's really happening in our hearts and minds is what truly builds authentic community.

So, what do you do to create a sustainable community, and how do you contribute to building it with and for others? I don't have many answers, but I do have some ideas.

First, decide who you want to be surrounded by. We're not necessarily looking to be entirely like-minded in everything, just like-minded in the important things. I'm not saying that if you're a tennis player, you should only create pockets of community with tennis players. However, if tennis is something that you place high value on, it would be important to become a part of a tennis club or a local court where the community plays tennis together. If you value your job and it has high importance in your life, I'm not saying surround yourself with only people who are obsessive over their work life (*I'm preaching to the choir!*), but it would be important to have a few friends who are willing

Married people can feel this too

to ask questions about your progress, push you toward the goals you want to achieve for yourself in this area, and encourage you along the way. Who do you want to be around?

Second, decide how you want to live your life. I have decided that I want to live my life abundantly, and being around a lot of people fills me up. What fills you up? How do you want to live your life? After my healing from shame and loneliness, I asked myself the question: *What do I want to spend my time doing*? It became abundantly clear that filling my time with people is what fills me up the most. We touched on this a few chapters ago in Friends with Babies, but if you value people, you will move mountains to build, maintain, and encourage friendships with them.

Third, if you don't have a natural community and you desire it, you have to build it. Have you ever seen the movie *Field of Dreams*? It's a 1989 sports fantasy drama where Ray Kinsella, played by Kevin Costner, builds a baseball diamond on his Iowa land. After the building is complete, ghosts of former baseball players emerge from the surrounding crops to come play ball. The famous quote from that film that Ray hears before he builds the Field of Dreams is, *"If you build it, they will come."* (Spoiler alert: Field of Dreams ends with every player who came to Ray's baseball diamond after death fulfilling their lost dreams.) It was one of my favorite movies as a child. With regard to community, if there is not already one for you: build it. I know it sounds daunting, and maybe it will be, but what if it's not? What if building the community you desire to be surrounded by changes your life? If you build it, they will come.

I'm not sure when we all first met, or what event spurred it on, but my small group is the best thing that's happened to me after Jesus and becoming an auntie. I remember sending a text after meeting with a friend for dinner one night, just throwing out an idea to a few girls locally who were around my same generation: *Did anyone want to go through a book together?* We were all navigating different life situations: some were married, others were unmarried, a few were dating, one was close to being engaged, a couple had kids, and the rest did not. A couple of women said they couldn't commit right now, and others responded delightedly. So, we forged ahead. The group that meets now is not the original group, but it is the group that is totally meant to do life together. And we do it well. We meet every single Thursday night. Mostly, we study the Bible, pray for and encourage each other, and sometimes enjoy cocktails. It's a group of nine women who are bonded not by a thread, but almost by super glue. We've seen each other through fire, especially the past few years. We have been together through seasons of extreme hardship, through seasons of pain, and through seasons of joy. We've *never stopped meeting together,* for years now, and the risk of the text message was worth the reward.

Are you the kind of person who hates a group text or the kind of person who loves a group text? I'm both. I both love and hate group texts. I love it when I need it, and I hate it when I'm in a meeting and come back to my phone filled with 303 unread messages. Well, our group text goes off all day long some days, and some days it's radio silent. But on days when someone is struggling, on days when someone needs prayer, on days when someone needs a friend, a dinner date, a book recommendation or simply a reminder that they are not alone in this fight of life, let me tell you who shows up: these girls. Inside of the group text and inside of real life, we are there for each other.

They're also each a monument of power in their own right. Some of us share the same chiropractor, whom we love and adore, and one day during a session he started asking questions about this group of friends.

"So let me get this straight—so-and-so has this kind of personality and is in Human Resources, so-and-so is passionate about healing for others, so-and-so is a Forensic Scientist who desperately seeks truth and applies it to daily life, so-and-so is in tech for luxury brands making life beautiful in ways for other people, so-and-so is building an app for one of the leading hotel companies in the nation for all kinds of people to experience travel at fair rates, and so-and-so works with children and so and so is in marketing for a major corporation and they're all really nice, every one of your friends who I've met is just so kind . . ." and the list went on and on and on. He wasn't associating their worth with their work, he was making the point that everyone was operating in their purpose and was really kind while they were doing it.

As he was speaking, I just nodded my head *yes* and responded in positive modifiers like "Mmhmm." When he was finished going through the list of my group of friends, he stopped what he was doing, looked at me and said, "You have successfully surrounded yourself with like-minded people. You're all Queen Bees." Feeling my heart swell with pride, I said, "You're so right. Everyone is doing exactly what they're supposed to be doing." Each woman is operating in the purpose that God has for her—the road marked out for her and her calling so sure. I felt so accomplished. And for once, it wasn't a conversation about who was married and who had babies. It was about who was walking in their respective purpose and contributing well to the world. One on-the-whim text several years prior had led this group of powerhouse women to engage in doing life together—grocery store trips, workout classes, birthday parties, fun seasons, and difficult ones—all the while, encouraging one another towards spiritual, relational, personal, and professional success. Just like the writer of Hebrews encouraged us to do: *spur one another on toward love and good deeds.*

I'm not saying your community will look exactly like mine. It won't, and in fact, I hope it doesn't—sometimes we're a mess. But I hope you are able to build a community that will grow with you. We are not created to live life alone. We need people in our lives who will encourage and challenge us. The lie is that that can only come from a spouse, the truth is that we are called to live a life in community regardless of our marital status.

Loneliness is one of the hardest feelings to combat, as far as I'm concerned. It feels safe to say that oftentimes the feeling that rises to the surface with shame is loneliness. Lonely is a liar. Lonely says, "No one likes you," and "It will feel like this forever." Lonely communicates fear, and maybe guilt, and, for some of us, a lot of questions. Will it always be this way? Does anyone like me? Am I not a good friend? How come I'm showing up for everyone, but it doesn't feel like anyone's showing up for me? Why is being unmarried in today's culture so painful, and why does it feel like something's wrong with me? One of the best parts about living with a community is that those fiery lies can be stomped on and extinguished immediately if you bring them to the surface. "I'm feeling lonely today—is anyone around to go for a walk or grab coffee?" is a text that has flown around our group several times. Sometimes people can and sometimes people can't, but when it's said aloud, the lie is met with truth and dissipates quickly.

No matter the reason, loneliness is a human condition—not a condition of being unmarried. Everyone experiences times of loneliness, and we all can learn how to cope healthily with this dilemma. Community is one of the most powerful ways that Christians in particular combat loneliness. Community is an incredible part of our growth as believers, and I would venture to say, potentially even our happiness. God created people, He loves people, and it is no surprise to Him that people need people. Community is important to our spiritual growth and development—and there is purpose in it.

What feelings bubble to the surface for you when thinking about community? It doesn't matter if you're introverted or extroverted; we're created for togetherness. If we're living a season of our lives unmarried, we must actively seek community, build it, and live life purposefully in it. But when we do, it's totally worth it. I promise. You are created to live and participate in thriving relationships with others.

With you especially now,
Megan

CREATED FOR COMMUNITY CHECKLIST

⬡ Make a list of the kind of people you'd like to be surrounded by and what you're looking for in community.

⬡ Decide how you want to live your life and what you'd like for it to feel like.

⬡ Join a local club or group of people who share your same interests.

⬡ If you're not in a small group, get in one! If you are, stay in one!

⬡ Take a walk and drink some water—consider inviting a friend.

CHAPTER 9

Where Do I Fit?

PITFALL THINKING

In the Christian world, I only matter
and have value if I am married.

PURPOSE THINKING

I have purpose and my
passions have value.

"For the kingdom of heaven is like a landowner who went out early in the morning to hire workers for his vineyard. He agreed to pay them a denarius[a] for the day and sent them into his vineyard. About nine in the morning he went out and saw others standing in the marketplace doing nothing. He told them, 'You also go and work in my vineyard, and I will pay you whatever is right.' So they went.

He went out again about noon and about three in the afternoon and did the same thing. About five in the afternoon he went out and found still others standing around. He asked them, 'Why have you been standing here all day long doing nothing?'

'Because no one has hired us,' they answered.

He said to them, 'You also go and work in my vineyard.'

When evening came, the owner of the vineyard said to his foreman, 'Call the workers and pay them their wages, beginning with the last ones hired and going on to the first.'

The workers who were hired about five in the afternoon came and each received a denarius. So when those who came were hired first, they expected to receive more. But each one of them also received a denarius. When they received it, they began to grumble against the landowner. 'These who were hired last worked only one hour,' they said, 'and you have made them equal to us who have borne the burden of the work and the heat of the day.'

But he answered one of them, 'I am not being unfair to you, friend. Didn't you agree to work for a denarius? Take your pay and go. I want to give the one who was hired last the same as I gave you. Don't I have the right to do what I want with my own money? Or are you envious because I am generous?'

So the last will be first, and the first will be last."

Matthew 20:1-16 NIV

Hey Contributor,

Can I be honest with you for a minute? This is where most of the ache comes in for me. Because our Christian culture is obsessed with marriage and babies and families, when we don't have our own, it is so easy to question our worth. It's simple to allow ourselves to believe that we don't matter or that we don't have a purpose in this season or in life, because that's often the message of the Christian world around us. How can we possibly contribute if we're not raising a family or cooking dinner for a husband every night? (*Ugh!*) It's so easy to fall into the trap of believing that we aren't contributing, that we aren't mature enough, that we haven't accomplished anything in our lives because we have yet to check these boxes off everyone else's list for us.

Please hear me clearly: You have purpose, you matter, and you are worthy, regardless of your relationship or familial status. No one has it harder or easier than anyone else because they are married with children or unmarried with no children or unmarried with children (although single parents are heroes, in my eyes!). We all are running the race marked out for us, regardless of who is or isn't running that race alongside us.

You have a lot to offer the world on your own, and having a companion doesn't mean you offer more or less. You are good, and you are worthy, and you are important just because you exist and have breath in your lungs. You have value because you have breath in your lungs. You are worthy of love because you are a human being with a heartbeat. Although that love doesn't always look how we think it should look, or want it to look, it does exist. Your value is not based on what you are contributing to the world, though we are called to contribute to the world. You see how tricky this line is? You are a whole person, valuable and worthy just as you are today. There is no part of you missing because you are unmarried.

The gifts, skills, and talents you possess are needed in the world. How do I know? You're here! You're breathing! Do you know what your giftings are? Frederick Buechner, American author, minister, theologian, and preacher wrote that "The place God calls you to is the place where your deep gladness and the world's deep hunger meet." What can't you stop thinking about? This is not a call to do something in the *meantime*; this is a call to do something *anyway*. Regardless of our marital or familial status, we are all contributors. We don't just participate in the contribution game when we have children or a husband; we participate in the contribution game anyway. This is not a *"what to do while we're waiting"* letter; this is a *"what we ought to do anyway"* song.

Buechner states, "Your deep gladness is the call of one's true, enduring and authentic self, the pursuits that engender, not necessarily always happiness, but profound joy." One thing of interest to note is that assuming where you fit is something we as Christians refer to as a calling—Buechner argues that that assumes a Caller. "There are all different kinds of voices calling you to all different kinds of work, and the problem is to find out which is the voice of God rather than of Society, say, or the Superego, or Self-Interest." The most important thing in discovering where we fit can arguably be: how connected are we to God? This is a rule of thumb remember, not exact science. The truest thing we can do in this season is stay in tune with the God who calls us to it all. Where do you have an uneasy spirit about the brokenness of this world? Where do you see that aligning with the heart of God? How can you take positive action to make a change for his Kingdom's purposes?

It all matters. Perhaps you are passionate about literacy and want to teach children to read, like my sister-in-law, or maybe you are passionate about nutrition and want to feed people who are hungry, like my friend Mona. Perhaps you feel so strongly about the world of addiction and suffering that you want to act in a tangible way, like our family friends who began a foundation that raises money to fight the disease of addiction to eradication. Maybe, like me, you're passionate about the poor in spirit and spend time dreaming of ways to make life more joyful. Where does a need meet your passion in the world?

There are women all over the world contributing to the work in God's vineyard in incredible ways. Married women and unmarried women alike are moving mountains so that the world spins on its axis. I know married women who are some of the best leaders in the workplace, unmarried women who are putting their whole self and tons of time into changing the world around them for better, unmarried women who are raising generations of future leaders by encouraging younger women to love and follow Jesus. There are married women who are some of the best business owners I know, making their neighborhoods and communities better. Do you see what I'm saying? Contribution doesn't have to do with being married or unmarried, and it's ridiculous for us to think that it does or for others to plant seeds that make us doubt our contributions. Your contribution matters and your labor in the Kingdom of God matters for eternity. We don't get into Heaven on the coattails of our potential husbands; we get into Heaven by recognizing, loving, and submitting to Jesus.

Where do you fit? Exactly where you are and contributing how you are. If you're in a place where you're not contributing to the betterment of the world around you and to the Kingdom of Jesus, I want to challenge you to get plugged in somewhere. Sign up to be an after-school tutor, help the single parent in your neighborhood with their kids after school, serve at a soup kitchen or food pantry and use your gifts to show the world the fullness of who God created you to be.

I have a friend who is unmarried. She is one of the most incredible contributors that I know. She has led women's ministry events with grace and charisma, visited sick friends, provided meals for those who are hungry. She serves on a leadership team, she hosts her friends, and she's an aunt to many of her local neighborhood kids. She's one of the most hospitable people I've ever encountered, she's constantly seeking how to make something better, and she is always willing to serve. It's like watching love in motion every time she walks through the door to an event or opens the door to her home. She doesn't need a counterpart to contribute, but if one day she does choose to get married, I know her husband will only enhance her ministry.

Another friend is lighting the world on fire right now with how she loves teenagers and serves their families relentlessly. She's serving in a local church as a full-time youth pastor and is one of the best in the game. She shows up—and that ministry, the one where presence takes precedent, speaks to the families she's serving. Volleyball games? She's there! Graduations? You can count on her! Days on the lake? She's your girl. She is leading small groups, serving students in practical ways, and investing in their lives way beyond a Sunday morning. She's discipling well and therefore contributing well. She does want to be married, and I'm praying God will provide that for her. In the meantime, though, she is sold out on contributing to the work in God's Kingdom and isn't just waiting until she has a counterpart to invest. She's the real deal, and I don't know anyone better.

We have the opportunity in this season to encourage others. We can contribute by seeing a need and filling it. We can reach out to schedule coffee dates and host our friends for dinner. The contributions we can make are endless—if we're operating in our gifting, calling, passion, and purpose.

An unmarried life offers itself to ask lots of questions. Does God truly have a plan for my life? If He does, is that plan as valuable as the plan for my friends who are married? This is where the Sovereignty of God comes into play. I have a mentor who taught me to rearrange my thinking. She says every time I am focused on the question "Why?" I need to replace it with the question "Can God be trusted?" The answer is a resounding yes, every single time.

Why some have the notion that unmarried women are second-class citizens is alarming, and perhaps even suggests that they believe God is not sovereign in His plan for our lives and cannot be trusted. The idea that unmarried women are incomplete and less valuable to God breaks His heart and ours. The Bible makes it clear that there is absolutely no second class when it comes to the people of God (Galatians 3:28).

Contributor, you are created in the image of God to accomplish His purposes. Marriage and children are not the only ways to serve and please a loving and kind God. Being married or unmarried doesn't give us value or decide whether we get to contribute. Being unmarried is good and so is being married, as long as we are focused on the mission and purpose God has for us in that season.

Kelly and I were on a run one steamy summer night. (You know Kelly, the one with the lists that rival mine and the reason for the checklists at the end of each chapter.) We were on the boardwalk in our hometown, watching surfers take wave after wave, mini golfers chasing their golf balls all over the course and teenagers Instagramming pictures of the sunset. We were on our fourth week of a running plan. She was killing it and I was suffering through it. I asked her questions about the season of life she had just come through, how it's relatable to unmarried women (although she is married with a baby!), and how the comparison trap continues to infiltrate even the strongest among us. She shared that we rank seasons in life based on how we feel about them and what our perspective is about that season. As a child, she wasn't the girl who always had the crush and wasn't particularly interested in chasing after boys on the playground. She didn't know if she would ever get married or not, and after becoming a Christian, was even more determined to live her life on mission. She said, "If I got married, it was because God had a mission for me and my husband within the context of our marriage, and if I didn't get married, it was because God had a mission for me outside of marriage."

Contributor, that's where our focus needs to remain. You have a mission, you have a purpose, and you have passions that matter to the existence of the world and to the advancement of God's Kingdom here on earth. If we get married, that's wonderful; it means that God has a mission for us within that marriage. If we don't get married, that's also wonderful; it means that God has a mission for us outside of marriage.

We must shift our focus, change our perspective, and help those around us change theirs as well. Marriage is not the goal; mission is the goal. Where are you at your best? You have purpose and your passions have value. Go get 'em!

I believe in you,
Megan

WHERE DO I FIT? CHECKLIST

⬡ Take a spiritual gifts assessment and meet with trusted friends or a pastor about the results.

⬡ If you're not already serving, decide where you will serve. How can you serve where you are?

⬡ Consider: Where would you like to be on a mission?

⬡ Ask someone to hold you accountable to staying the course of your mission.

⬡ Take a walk and drink some water.

CHAPTER 10

Where Is God?

PITFALL THINKING

I am forgotten by God.

PURPOSE THINKING

He sees and knows me intimately.

Hey you,

Are you familiar with the story of Abraham and Isaac in the Bible? As a refresher, when Abraham was 99 years old, God promised him and his wife, Sarah, then 89, a son. You read that right: 89 and 99 years old and expecting a child. Here's the story:

> "God also said to Abraham, 'As for Sarai your wife, you are no longer to call her Sarai; her name will be Sarah. I will bless her and will surely give you a son by her. I will bless her so that she will be the mother of nations; kings of peoples will come from her.' Abraham fell facedown; he laughed and said to himself, 'Will a son be born to a man a hundred years old? Will Sarah bear a child at the age of ninety?' Then God said, 'Yes, your wife Sarah will bear you a son, and you will call him Isaac. I will establish my covenant with him as an everlasting covenant for his descendants after him . . .'" Genesis 17:15-19 NIV

Finally, the thing Abraham and Sarah wanted most in the world was happening. Sarah became pregnant and had a son with Abraham, at the very moment it had been predicted. Abraham, then one hundred years old, named the child Isaac. When Isaac was young, God told Abraham, "Take your son, your only son, Isaac, whom you love, and go to the region of Moriah. Sacrifice him there as a burnt offering on one of the mountains I will tell you about" (Genesis 22:2).

I'M SORRY, WHAT?! Could you imagine hearing that from God? You've begged and pleaded and prayed for this thing for so long, and he gives it to you, and now He needs you to give it back. Not only does He need you to give it back, but He asks you to sacrifice it at His altar. We can only imagine the bewilderment and shock Abraham must have felt. He probably thought, "Surely, that can't be right!" And yet, even with his doubts, he started packing.

> "Abraham took Isaac, two servants, and a donkey and set off on the 50-mile journey. When they arrived, Abraham told the servants to wait with the donkey while he and Isaac went up the mountain. He told the men, 'We will worship and then we will come back to you.'" Genesis 22:5b

Isaac asks his dad where the lamb was for the sacrifice, and Abraham answers that the Lord will provide the lamb. I don't know this for sure, but given the context of what we do know, I am guessing that a grief-stricken and terribly confused Abraham tied Isaac with ropes and placed him on the altar before him.

Just as Abraham raised the knife to kill his son, the angel of the Lord called out to Abraham to stop! The angel said he knew that Abraham feared the Lord because he had not withheld his only son, the thing he had wanted most.

Insane obedience. When Abraham looked up, he saw a ram caught in a thicket by its horns. He sacrificed the animal provided by God, instead of his son. Then the angel of the Lord called to Abraham and said:

> "I swear by myself, declares the LORD, that because you have done this and have not withheld your son, your only son, I will surely bless you and make your descendants as numerous as the stars in the sky and as the sand on the seashore. Your descendants will take possession of the cities of their enemies, and through your offspring all nations on earth will be blessed, because you have obeyed me." Genesis 22:16-18

Abraham obeyed God. In the middle of incredible heartbreak, he kept choosing obedience. Isaac was the thing he wanted most in the world, God gave him Isaac, and then asked for him right back. And yet Abraham obeyed—right away and all the way. Isaac would go on to become an important character in the biblical narrative: the father of Jacob, whose twelve sons would become the twelve tribes of Israel, and eventually the patriarch of all the Israelites.

While God has not asked us to sacrifice our children at an altar, I'm certain that we have fought through seasons of laying all sorts of Isaacs on the altar of the Lord. All the things we want most in the world require allowing Jesus to take them back from us—out of our grip and out of our control. I'm wondering if you're reading this with tears in your eyes, like I am writing it. The thing that maybe we want most in the world, to be married, to attain a certain level of success, to be on a mission we're not on yet, just is not happening for us. So, what do we do?

Maybe our perfect worlds, which we once thought were secure, safe, and comfortable, became wildly disrupted by trial after trial and potentially even some tremendous heartbreak. Confusion, frustration, and hurt may have led the way into our last few trips around the sun, while joy, peace, and love took a back seat.

Our fierce grip of control on our lives has been thwarted by the plans of God, and He is using this season to peel our fingers away ever-so-gently from things that we're clinging to instead of Him.

Lay your Isaacs down, Megan. Give them to Me, I journaled through tears one morning. *I don't know why you're asking for these things back,* I wrote. *This is so painful.*

I know. Trust Me.

Abraham was righteous and obedient, unlike me. Yikes. He had one Isaac to lay down—one person he loved so much that it completely broke his heart to give back to God. In my Isaacs season, God was asking me to trust Him only and to give Him back what wasn't mine to start with. These were things God was calling me to give back to Him, to lay at His altar, to let go of in order to be more obedient to His calling and His plans for my life. I had dreamed of a life with a husband and family for so long and it seemed to become the only thing I could focus on worth accomplishing. He was asking me to give that back to Him. There are other things we may give back to Him, too: our ideal job situations, career advancements, dreams that don't seem to be coming true no matter how hard we try. The health of someone we love or the thoughts of what we pictured our current life to be are also things we should consider placing on His altar. What is He asking you to lay down?

Everything I once thought was, wasn't . . . and on this side of that season, I know I am better for it. My heart has been turned inside out, cleaned, made new, expanded, and then set back inside of me. Friendships, relationships, ministry, good plans—all very good gifts and all very terrible gods. When I worship things that aren't Him, when I pay more attention to voices that aren't His, when I cling tightly to stuff that doesn't respect His will—He asks me to give it back. Every time. Whose voice are you listening to, sweet friend? Where is your God?

Laying down our Isaacs means that we give back to God the things we value most. Friendships, relationships, family, money, big plans, dreams, hopes, and hurts—and that's just the short list.

Even experiencing incredible misery as we've traveled up our own Mount Moriah, it's probably safe to assume that we're wondering if He'd really call us to give it back once we get there. I bet sometimes He has . . .

. . . and each time we're better for it.

. . . and each time we're stronger because of it.

. . . and each time we can choose to see through a beautiful lens of trust that allows us to know Him more.

This is right where we want to be because otherwise, we are complete disasters. We will climb Mount Moriah every single time if it means we get to be that much closer to the Creator and Sustainer of our life.

Which of your Isaacs do you need to lay down? What are you clinging too tightly to that isn't Jesus? Controlling Megan is now in recovery and can tell you that the other side of sacrifice is better. It is a life of obedience.

He sees and knows you intimately. You are created for a purpose that He knows.

In it,
Megan

WHERE IS GOD?
CHECKLIST

◇ Read the story of Abraham and Sarah in your favorite translation of the Bible.

◇ Write a letter to God about how you're feeling in this season of life.

◇ Spend five silent minutes with God. Ask Him a question and wait for the answer.

◇ Decide on a new devotional book or Bible study that you'd like to do. For low-cost ideas, borrow from friends, your church, or local library.

◇ Take a walk and drink some water.

CHAPTER 11

Pursuing Peace

PITFALL THINKING

When my life doesn't look how I thought
it should look at this point, everything
seems chaotic.

PURPOSE THINKING

We can seek peace and pursue it.

Hey Cool Kid,

Chaos. Insanity. Whirlwind. Tornado. "What in the world?!" Anxiety. Madness. Turmoil. Commotion. Havoc.

Words that people are using to describe the current state of our world are all synonyms of each other, each linked to the other by their disdain for peace. Have you ever felt that way?

While I am interested in the affairs of the world, I am more interested in our *response* to the affairs of the world. We've watched and listened as our inner thoughts have amplified the good, the bad, and the ugly. We've journaled and prayed and thought about why we respond the way we do to certain situations, especially ones that we have no control over. And there is the answer: *control.*

Admittedly, I am a recovering hyper-active control freak. I have been freed from that burden after a lot of hard work! It took a while for me to uncover the why of this ugly attribute, but once I did, freedom was mine. Does it still creep in sometimes? Sure. Do I know what to do when it comes? Absolutely!

The process of pursuing peace and relinquishing control can become the soundtrack by which we live our lives. Control is about us. It tries to convince us that we have a say over every single step; when pursuing peace is about responding to the purpose Jesus has for our lives.

Control says, "I don't trust You," while Peace responds, "I have the best plans for you." Control says, "My way is the best way!" while Peace responds, "Actually . . . MY way is the best way." Control says, "You don't know the right way," while Peace responds, "I am the way."

When our world feels like absolute chaos, we have a choice: Will we control the things that are not ours to control? Or will we surrender it all to Him whose ways are best, whose thoughts are higher, and whose peace is immeasurable? We must choose to surrender.

Married women to

We go into control hyper-drive when things don't go our way, when we've planned something that gets canceled, or when someone in a position of authority above us says, "Actually, we have to do it like this now instead." If we are not actively pursuing peace during all of this worldly chaos, it will end very ugly for us. How, as unmarried women, will we respond to a world of internal chaos when our entire lives aren't panning out how we originally thought they would? How will we be women of peace and purpose, instead of women of chaos and calamity?

The choice is ours.

Jesus says directly to us in the Gospel of Matthew, "Come to me, all you who are weary and burdened, and I will give you rest."

The hard truth today, friends, is that we will not find rest and peace while we hold on to control. We only find true rest and peace in absolute surrender to Him.

Are you burdened? Weary? Heavy-hearted? Try saying this out loud: "Jesus, I give this thing to you (whatever your thing is) because it's exhausting me and I'm asking you to take care of it. I surrender."

Now, take a deep breath.
Unclench your fist.
Relax your jaw line.
. . . another deep breath.
Lower your shoulders.

It's all His to handle anyway, sweet friend. Just give it back to Him. Life is sweet on the side of surrender.

In her Bible study, *Create in Me a Heart of Peace*, Becky Keife says this, "In the aftermath of 9/11 and in the wake of (a) devastating breakup, God was inviting me to change the way I defined peace and change where I look for it. Living in a prosperous first world country is no guarantee of peace. Peace doesn't come from titles like boyfriend and girlfriend. Peace is not found in relationships or plans unfolding according to my dreams. That heartbreaking (season) showed me that the peace the world gives is temporary, circumstantial, fallible. But God offers a different kind of peace. Lasting. Unshakeable. Perfect. When the whole world fractures or my own life shatters, the peace of Jesus is still available because the person of Jesus never changes. Whether we're in a time of crisis or just trudging through the struggles of ordinary life, we can entrust our troubled, fearful hearts to the one who is worthy of our trust."

If we are looking at our circumstances or the people in our circumstances to provide lasting peace for us, we are looking in the wrong place. Jesus is the only place to find peace—not because of what He does but simply because of who He is. Are you looking for peace in your unmarried life? It can be found in the person of Jesus.

or married

Freedom from Suffering

I missed the phone call. I was loading the dishwasher and to be honest, I didn't even hear it. I called back and without a single "Hello?" on the other end, I heard these words: "Can you help me? I don't know what's going on. I feel . . . awful."

My friend began to describe her plight through some moments of panic and anxiety laced with depressive thoughts, and I couldn't tell her what she wanted me to tell her. She wanted me to say, "It's okay. You can make it; these feelings will end on _____ date." But I couldn't tell her that. I could only offer a listening ear, some prayer, and lots of questions to try to get to the root.

I could offer hope in the form of: "This will end; I know it will."

But I couldn't tell her when.

I could offer empathy in the form of: "I understand how painful this is."

But I couldn't change her situation.

I could offer guidance in the form of: "You keep doing what you're doing. I'm going to pray right now."

But I couldn't take the pain away from her. It was heartbreaking enough to listen to, and my mind took me right back to the time when

I lived similarly—always looking for the out, the end date, the concrete answer of when I would be okay again.

Rewind thousands of years and we see this same pain echoed in the story of another woman in the Bible.

It took 105,192 hours to be exact. For twelve years, this woman bore the emotional and psychological baggage of being unclean and untouchable. No hugs, kisses, or any type of intimacy with a husband (if she had one). She could not prepare her family's food (if she even had one). She could not do housework (if she had a home). She couldn't be a wife (if she was married). She couldn't be a mommy (if she had children). She had sat in an isolated house for twelve years staring at the walls. For all intents and purposes, she was as good as invisible.

She was a woman with an issue of blood in a culture, religion and nation that deemed her unclean because of it. But then she hears about Jesus. He comes to her town. He's healed others. She believes He can heal her, too. She hopes that He can.

She experienced twelve years of no answers, of wanting healing, twelve years of waiting, twelve years of wishing, twelve years of the same draining health issues. 105,192 hours of suffering. The story goes like this:

> "When Jesus had again crossed over by boat to the other side of the lake, a large crowd gathered around him while he was by the lake. Then one of the synagogue leaders, named Jairus, came, and when he saw Jesus, he fell at his feet. He pleaded earnestly with him, 'My little daughter is dying. Please come and put your hands on her so that she will be healed and live.' So, Jesus went with him. A large crowd followed and pressed around him. And a woman was there who had been subject to bleeding for twelve years. She had suffered a great deal under the care of many doctors and had spent all she had, yet instead of getting better, she grew worse. When she heard about Jesus, she came up behind him in the crowd and

touched his cloak, because she thought, 'If I just touch his clothes, I will be healed.' Immediately, her bleeding stopped, and she felt in her body that she was freed from her suffering.

At once, Jesus realized that power had gone out from him. He turned around in the crowd and asked, 'Who touched my clothes?'

'You see the people crowding against you,' his disciples answered, 'and yet you can ask, "Who touched me?"' But Jesus kept looking around to see who had done it. Then the woman, knowing what had happened to her, came and fell at his feet and, trembling with fear, told him the whole truth. He said to her, 'Daughter, your faith has healed you. Go in peace and be freed from your suffering.'" Mark 5:21-34 NIV

Twelve straight years of the same suffering and pain, yet she persisted. She never gave up hoping that one day maybe she would be clean. Twelve straight years of many doctors and likely spending all the money she had, only to receive little to no answers.

But then . . . Jesus.

She shouldn't have even been in the crowd in the first place because she was deemed unclean by her society, yet she persisted in her pursuit of Him.

I love that this specific story allows us to know her innermost thoughts: "If I just touch his clothes, I will be healed." She was a determined woman. So, she ran after Him, she pursued Him, and she persisted in her act of seeking healing from the true source. Her sickness did not have the last word.

"Daughter, your faith has healed you. Go in peace and be freed from your suffering."

Where are you suffering today, friend? Where do you need freedom? Are you wondering where God is throughout a painful situation when you so badly want something you're not getting?

Run after Him, find Him, push through crowds to get to Him, just reach out for a little bit of Him, pursue Him, seek Him, and exhaust yourself pushing for Him and only Him. This world will break our hearts ten ways to Sunday, but He will never. Our healing from whatever suffering we're facing can only and ever be found in Him.

When you find Him, however you find Him, He will have the final word to your suffering and pain and wondering where He is.

You will live an abundant life on this earth because of Him. You will see the goodness of the Lord in the land of the living. You will know His presence and His grace and His goodness in your life.

"Go in peace and be free." He sees and knows you intimately.

I'm not sure where God is in every season and why life can feel seemingly chaotic when we don't get what we want, when things get difficult, when there are storms or chaos. I've asked the same questions that you've been asking. What I do know is that surrendering to His will, instead of fighting it, is one of the most beautiful experiences of my life to date.

Since learning to surrender to Him that marriage is not the entire goal of my life—in ways like choosing to be okay with what's happening in my life, pursuing my purpose regardless of my relationship status, and reframing my mindset, I've heard "You're glowing! Are you in love?!" more times than I can count. I almost wish I was kidding, because that feels like a hard thing to hear when you're not actually in love—except that my friends mean it as a compliment. I love glowing in the world, shining even though my life is not exactly how I thought it would be. Peace looks good on us.

When I was in the thick of my pitfall season, I read a thread on Twitter. (That in and of itself is dangerous, I know.) It was an entire thread dedicated to women who are unmarried and wanting to be, especially women who place themselves in the Christian camp. The thread discussed the difficulties that this situation brings upon us and there was a lot of camaraderie between the person who posted and those replying.

One thing she stated was that she just wanted to "experience the peace of being chosen." It was the most relatable thing I'd read on this topic in a long time. That's all I wanted, the peace of being chosen.

In her book *Holier Than Thou*, Jackie Hill Perry writes "One who knows all things and controls all things cannot and will not be troubled by what He has infinite knowledge of and complete sovereignty over. Underneath human anxiety is the reversal of identity in which the finite attempts to be infinite. With our finite knowledge, we want to know everything so as to not be caught off guard by anything. With our finite abilities, we want and try to control everything so we're not controlled by anything. We fail to do both because it's impossible to be like God in this way, making the peace of God elusive for those who need it most. But behold Jesus. He is forever settled, unshaken, and unbothered to the point that he can sleep like a baby while a storm rages war on his resting place. Being the Creator of it and the Lord over it, He commands the storm to do what He has always had and what He is never hesitant to give, 'Peace! Be Still!'"

What I think happened is that I experienced the glow after surrendering to His will and realizing that I was already chosen, and so are you. We are both chosen by a God who loves us and sees us and has plans for our lives that are more meaningful than anything we could ever make up in our wildest dreams and chosen by a God who is Peace and continues to give us Himself every day. Just be still.

God is with you, and He is choosing you in this season. Choose Him back. Seek peace and pursue it. There, you will experience the glow. I promise.

Pursuing with you,
Megan

PURSUING PEACE CHECKLIST

○ Read the story of the woman with the issue of blood in your favorite translation of the Bible. (Mark 5:21-34)

○ Write down a list of things that need peace in your life—where do you need to see God move?

○ Decide to move towards something instead of away from something. What's your purpose? Pursue it!

○ When you fall into the pit of chaos, think about something that will bring you peace in that moment and do it! Music? Book? Walk? Call someone?

○ Take a walk and drink some water.

CHAPTER 12

So Now What?

PITFALL THINKING

I don't have a purpose.

PURPOSE THINKING

Of course, I do! It's just a different
"I do!" than I expected.

Beloved,

It was Thanksgiving Day and my family was seated around the table at my parent's house, the home my brothers and I grew up in and the place where we all still gather regularly. My mom and dad work hard to make sure that every holiday is special and every event feels fun and exciting, especially for their grandchildren. My mom, retired from kindergarten special education, decided that this particular Thanksgiving would be filled with a lot of meaningful conversation. She and my dad filled an entire fishbowl with questions we were to answer throughout the meal.

It was my little brother's turn to choose a question out of the fishbowl. He grabbed the sliver of paper and read aloud: "If you could give everyone in the world one thing, what would you give them?"

Everyone started to respond in practical ways—"I'd make sure everyone had enough financing for every basic need," or, "I'd give everyone three nutritious meals a day," or "I'd give everyone something fun!"

Evan, my younger brother, sat in silence listening to everyone answer this question that was really his to answer. "Alright, your turn," someone said.

After putting his fork down, taking a deep breath, and looking around at all of us, Evan calmly stated: "Purpose. I would make sure that everyone knew their purpose." The table grew quiet. My mom's eyes filled with tears, and my dad just shook his head.

"Yup," our older brother exclaimed, "you win." We could feel his answer permeate the air waves around us and we knew he was right. While we were busy thinking about the tangible, he was busy thinking about the heart. What will keep us going? Purpose.

According to the Oxford Languages Dictionary, purpose is *the reason for which something is done or created, or for which something* *exists.* Friend, you are created in the image of God in order to accomplish His purposes. Marriage and children are not the only ways to serve and please a loving and kind God. Being married or unmarried isn't the thing that gives us value and allows us to participate in the abundant full life or not. Remember, single life is good and so is marriage, as long as we are focused on the mission and purpose God has for us in that season.

In interviewing women for the content of this book, it became abundantly clear that we have set our expectations on things that don't matter in this life. Who we are matters; how we respond to a broken, hurting, and needy world matters; how we speak to our friends, colleagues, neighbors, and family matters—not whether we do that with or without a ring on our finger. It was heartbreaking to receive the responses of so many women who felt no value or who felt undervalued because of their marital status.

Viola Davis is an American actress and producer. She is the recipient of various accolades, including an Academy Award, a Primetime Emmy Award, and two Tony Awards; she is the only African American to achieve the Triple Crown of Acting. She is quoted as saying, "Do not live someone else's life and someone else's idea of what womanhood is. Womanhood is you. Womanhood is everything that's inside of you." It's apparent that what has happened to us—unmarried women, women with no children, or women who don't fit into a category that church culture has created for us—is that we've been so busy trying to live up to the expectations others have set for us that we forget to just live, for our God and for our purpose.

Your life is filled with purpose. Big ones, sure, but also small ones. There is purpose in your running and doing, in your seeing and being. There is purpose in your errands, in your visiting friends and family, and in your paying bills. There is purpose in your work, and your mission, and your neighborhood. There is purpose in the pit, in the dreams, in coming out of shame and in owning our spot in this life. There is purpose for you in your family, in the lives of your friends and community. You fit exactly where you are supposed to fit—exactly where you are. You are filled with possibility because you are filled with purpose.

So, what?

So, what do we do when we feel like God is cheating *us* while blessing *them*? Or what do we do when we're content with our beautiful life? We choose to believe that God is a God full of plans for us, full of goodness for us, and full of abundance for us. The moment that we're in does not change the ultimate mission that we're on. The pinnacle of the human experience is to walk with God and live in love with Him and His people.

The Psalmist writes, "The Lord directs the steps of the godly. He delights in every detail of their lives. Though they stumble, they will never fall, for the Lord holds them by the hand" (Psalm 37:23-24). We have the best hand-holder walking us along our path of purpose and it will never be purposeless if we're walking it with Him.

Matthew Henry's Concise Commentary on the Whole Bible unpacks this passage in such a beautiful way that we can apply it to our lives right away. Henry writes, "The blessing of God is the spring, sweetness, and security of all earthly enjoyments. And if we are sure of this, we are sure not to want anything good for us in this world. By his grace and Holy Spirit, he directs the thoughts, affections, and designs of good men. By his providence he overrules events, so as to make their way plain. He does not always show them his way for a distance, but leads them step-by-step, as children are led." If we are sure of this, of God's blessing and hand in our lives, we will not want for anything good in this world. We will be so busy enjoying the *now* that we won't be focused on the ever-present reminder of what is not or not yet.

Later in the Psalms, the Psalmist continues, "But you would be fed with the finest of wheat; with honey from the rock I would satisfy you" (Psalm 81:16). Meaning, that God provides everything we need, even from the sources and the situations where we least expect it. Who among us thought our lives would turn out exactly how they are? But God. He fed the Israelites honey from the rock, too. He always shows up in the least expected places, with the best gifts. We see this in Moses' song in Deuteronomy 32 where he spoke as a witness against a rebellious Israel as he was reminding them of God's faithfulness to them. We are reminded here about the sweetness of honey. God's love doesn't want us to survive only with what's essential: He can also give us sweetness in the whatever context the Spirit drives us. God wants us to experience the sweetness of life with Him regardless of our marital status. Are you looking for honey in the rock, too? I know I am. Pursue the sweetness, regardless of who is in the season with you. Your life is beautiful, good, and purposeful. You are experiencing exactly what you are supposed to experience with a God who has the best plans for you. He gave a wandering Israel honey from a rock; He can provide anything for you!

Do you know the song "You'll Never Walk Alone," originally written and released in 1963 by Gerry and the Peacemakers? They sing:

"When you walk through a storm, hold your head up high and don't be afraid of the dark.

At the end of a storm, there's a golden sky and the sweet silver song of a lark.

Walk on through the wind, walk on through the rain for your dreams be tossed and blown.

Walk on, walk on with hope in your heart and you'll never walk alone.

You'll never walk alone,

Walk on, walk on with hope in your heart and you'll never walk alone

You'll never walk alone."

Beloved, you are not alone. You have more purpose than I could fill these pages with. Your walk is one of power, significance, righteousness, and blessing. I know being unmarried in the Christian culture feels kind of stormy, so hold your head up high and don't be afraid of the dark. There's a promise for us as we cling to Jesus and His purposes for our lives. It can be found all throughout the Bible, in our conversations with people who love us, and in a song released in 1963: Walk on with hope in your heart and you'll never walk alone.

So *now* what? Go. Live! The journey doesn't have to look exactly how we thought it would be to be good and filled with joy. God didn't get it wrong, beloved. He got it all one hundred percent right—He always has, and He always will. I heard a pastor once say that worry is the fear that God is going to get it wrong, bitterness is believing that He did. We are not called to live in the bitter; we are called to live in the better. He has so much more for you. And as it turns out, your life of freedom and abundance is actually happily ever after, after all.

I've been praying for you as I've been writing this—and even now as you're reading it, my prayer has not changed. May you find your purpose and operate in its fullness, regardless of your marital status. You are not less than, you are not almost-someone, you are not lacking anything. You are just enough; you are filled to the brim with opportunities to create and laugh and dance and engage and worship and guide and shape and mold and encourage and be exactly who you are supposed to be. You are not worth more with a spouse at your side. You are worth exactly what Jesus thought you were worth from the very beginning of time—everything.

Let's live,
Megan

SO NOW WHAT? CHECKLIST

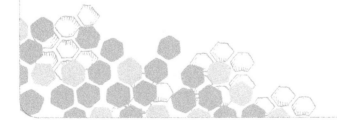

○ LIVE!

○ And while you're at it—take a walk and drink some water.

Acknowledgments

It feels like maybe this should be a speech at an awards show, but there are some people that deserve to be acknowledged at the completion of this book. First, **Jesus**, my first love and greatest relationship. Thank you for saving my life. Second only to Jesus is **my (whole big, wild) family**: you are my strength, support, and backbone. Thank you for pushing me! I cannot believe we belong to each other. Your love infiltrates every fiber of my being and I love life with you. **Lakay Papa M', Lumiere et Paix & Dayspring Ministries Haiti**, *Mwen renmen ou! Ou se fanmi mwen. Mèsi pou kè kontan!* **Christy,** thank you for helping me get unstuck, for pushing me to write, and asking a lot of questions every single day. Our entire lives you've been my champion; life with you is one of my greatest joys. I don't deserve your friendship. Thank you for being my best best friend. Continuing in the influential people category come **Craig & Nancy,** and **Kathryn**, this is your inheritance. You are the real deal. Fast isn't the Kingdom. Thank you for loving a lost fifteen-year-old.

And then I grew up a little bit. While my family, Christy, the Markers, and Kathryn continued to pour their lives into mine, **Amanda, Kate, Jenna** came along to teach me more about vulnerability. You are the sisters of my heart and I'll love you forever for it. **Kate**—I cannot believe that we got to walk through this season of publishing together. What a dream, and of course, how hilarious. Shortly after Amanda, Jenna, and Kate brought me back to life, the **Thursday Night Girl Gang** arrived on the scene—*Deanna, Elisabeth, Jen, Kory, Lanie, Sami, Shanna, Victoria*: Your sisterhood in this season has been unlike anything I have ever experienced. Thank you for celebrating, crying, praying, and encouraging me. Here's to all our dreams being realized for the rest of our lives! I love doing life with you. Buzz buzz. **Molly & Amy,** thank you for praying with me, crying with me, and laughing with me. I love everything about all that we are and have. Thank you. **Nonie**, I would not be here without you. Thank you is an understatement. To **Natalie, Karen, Diane, Jess, Heather, Nancy, Alicia, Kyle, Kelly, Emilie, Tasha and Nadine**, your guidance love, championing, and big sister support is unmatched. I am so grateful for your presence in my life. Thank you for being you and supporting me and this book so well. Thank you to **SPOGC Staff, Community, and Anchored Families** for championing me in writing this book and full-time ministry at the same time. Your grace is kind. And to **Shanna and Joey**, thank you for *The War of Art* by Steven Pressfield and your *"Give us what you've got!"*—I've thought about that every day while completing this project. And to **Rachel, Kristy, Jess, Nikki, Sam**, and all the friends all over the place who have walked with me, cried with me, prayed with me, encouraged me, and poured your life into mine—thank you! If I were to name every person, this entire book would only be names. Thank you, thank you, thank you.

While those relationships are incredibly meaningful to me, this book would not be possible without the work of others. **Ariel Curry**, you are, by far, the best editor in the whole big wide world. Thank you for your kindness, your patience, your grace, your willingness, your questions, your time, your answers, your advice, your encouragement, your *"Megan, you have what it takes"* pep talks while I cried, your backspace to take out every extra space between sentences, and your championing of this book. I cannot thank you enough, Ariel. Thank you for introducing me to **Mandy and the entire team at MRM—Sara, Randi, Nelly, Melissa, Carol**—who I owe a lot to. Working with you on this project has been grace-filled, loving, kind, and everything I didn't know the publishing world could be. You are the best in the business, and I am forever grateful for your care and friendship in this publishing project. Thank you, each of you. To **Analiese, Diane, Kate, Kelly L, Kyle,** I still can't believe you read the ugliest version of this book that existed. Your kindness is something I will never forget. Thank you for your honesty, your encouragement, and your compassion. I love you! **Kelly,** especially for every run, every brainstorming session, every incentive writing, every time you jumped right in when I felt like I couldn't think of one more word—you are a gem. Thank you. I owe you! **Jenna Shotmeyer,** thank you, friend, for your encouragement and kindness, your coaching, and your championing. You're the best. To **Kristine**, who never signed up to be my sounding board but just to be my friend—I cannot thank you enough. Your insight is wise, and I am so grateful for you.

And to the **women who graciously took their time to be interviewed** as I was carefully weaving thoughts together to put into writing, your insight is the most valuable to me. This book is for you. Thank you for answering questions and responding in text and e-mail and on Instagram stories. The information you so willingly shared has more value than I could ever tell you in words. Thank you.

The thing about this book is that it isn't necessarily filled with new ideas, just ones that are written down. Thank you, to the **readers**, for reading. I will never be able to express enough gratitude.

About the Author

Megan Faulkner is an author, podcaster, and speaker, who engages the world with authenticity, wit, and Biblical Truth. Megan has invested more than 15+ years serving the local church in student ministry, walking with teenagers and their families through all of the fun (and tough!) stuff of life. She is especially passionate about seeing people experience the love of Jesus and leave radically changed—whether those people are teenagers, women, the outcast, or Haitian orphans.

Megan loves serving on the leadership board for Dayspring Ministries Haiti, where she's responsible for any tasks that come her way. Dayspring resources over 50 churches, 25 schools, an orphanage, a widow's and young mother's program, a clean water initiative, a micro-loan program, and is entirely staffed by Haitian nationals and American volunteers.

As an avid communicator, Megan can be found hanging out on Instagram @meganefaulk, or on her Podcast, Wife Me Up, which is available on all podcast streaming platforms. Aside from the passions that ministry brings her way, Megan can also often be found on the beach or entertaining friends in her home—two of her favorite things. In addition to communicating, she enjoys a life filled with motion. Swimming, biking, and suffering through running are some of her favorite activities compounded into the sport of Triathlon— which she loves.

You can find out more and get connected with Megan at
www.meganefaulkner.com.

Notes

Introduction

Oxford English Dictionary. 2013. Oxford University Press.

Chapter 1: Stuck in the Pit

"Stuck." https://www.vocabulary.com/dictionary/stuck

Downs, Annie F. https://instagram.com/anniefdowns

Chapter 3: Shame

Brown, Brene. "Shame V. Guilt." https://Brenebrown.Com/
Articles/2013/01/15/Shame-v-guilt/. January 15, 2013.

Chapter 6: FWB: Friends with Babies

Dr. Edith Eger. *"Recognizing the Choices and Gifts in Our Lives."*
Brene Brown's *Unlocking Us* Podcast. Spotify, 2021.

Chapter 8: Created for Community

Field of Dreams. Gordon Company, 1989.

Chapter 9: Where Do I Fit?

Buechner, Frederick. 1993. *Wishful Thinking: A Seeker's ABC*.
HarperOne.

Chapter 11: Pursuing Peace

Keife, Becky. 2022. *Create in Me A Heart of Peace*. Revell.

Perry, Jackie H. 2021. *Holier Than Thou: How God's Holiness Helps Us Trust Him*. B&H Books.

Chapter 12: So Now What?

Oxford English Dictionary. 2013. Oxford University Press.

Davis, Viola. "#AskHerMore: 11 Empowering Messages From Inspiring Women On The Red Carpet At The Oscars." Https://Www.Huffingtonpost.Co.Uk/2015/02/24/Ask-her-more-empowering-women-red-carpet_n_6741524.Html. February 25, 2015.

Henry, Matthew. 2003. *Matthew Henry's Concise Commentary on the Whole Bible*. Thomas Nelson.

Gerry and the Peacemakers. *"You'll Never Walk Alone."* 1963.

CPSIA information can be obtained
at www.ICGtesting.com
Printed in the USA
BVHW032119140423
662383BV00001B/1

9 798986 802367